THE MAGNA CARTA
OF CHESHIRE

Graeme J. White

With a Translation of the Charter by Jonathan Pepler

Published by the Cheshire Local History Association,
c/o Cheshire Archives and Local Studies,
Duke Street, Chester, CH1 1RL,
2015.

A catalogue record for this book is available from the British Library.

ISBN 978-1-905702-78-7

Front cover: A sixteenth-century representation of the earl of
Chester presiding over a meeting of his lay and ecclesiastical
barons (Cheshire Archives & Local Studies, ZCX/2), first
published in Daniel King's *The Vale Royal of England* in
1656. This is reproduced by kind permission of Cheshire
Archives & Local Studies. There is no historical foundation
for the picture, which shows the first earl, Hugh d'Avranches,
in company with the mitred abbots of religious houses which
were not founded until after his death. However, the image
does capture an enduring belief within Cheshire about the
relative autonomy of its medieval governmental
arrangements, with the earl standing in place of the king: a
belief fostered in part by the issue, and then the repeated
confirmation and referencing, of the county's own Magna
Carta.

Printed by Doppler Press, Hockley, Essex

PREFACE

It was Doug Haynes, former chairman of Cheshire Local History Association and still a member of the Executive Committee, who suggested to the Association that the Magna Carta of Cheshire deserved more attention. We have been happy to oblige with what is, in effect, the county's contribution to the 800th anniversary celebrations of the events at Runnymede in June 1215.

The 'Cheshire Magna Carta' was already being described by the end of the thirteenth century as 'the common charter of Cheshire'. As such, it is a document which every resident of the county should know about and can take some pride in. It is also a document of significance for regional and national history. Our intention has been, through a new translation and an accompanying commentary, to make it more accessible and to enhance its contribution to our understanding of medieval law, politics, landscape, society and economy, within the county and beyond.

We are grateful to the Association for agreeing to publish this short book and to several fellow-scholars for their enthusiastic support and most helpful advice, among them Dr Paul Booth, Ms Rachel Swallow and Professors Stephen Church, Edmund King and Nicholas Vincent. Responsibility for the translation and accompanying analysis is, of course, entirely our own. We hope that they will be of interest to everyone who shares our enthusiasm for the history of a very special county.

Jonathan Pepler
Graeme White

January 2015

CONTENTS

Introduction

Sometime in 1215 or 1216, probably in the weeks following King John's consent to the terms of Magna Carta at Runnymede beside the Thames in mid-June 1215, Ranulf III earl of Chester granted a charter in the county court of Cheshire containing several concessions to his barons.[1] Known to historians as the Magna Carta of Cheshire - indeed, already being described in such terms during the thirteenth century - the document has only thirteen 'clauses' dealing with various issues and is thus much shorter than the king's iconic charter, which has 63.[2] Nevertheless, some of the clauses echo those in the Runnymede Magna Carta. There is, for example, the same concern to provide protection against arbitrary treatment of widows and the heirs to estates and a parallel undertaking that concessions made to the barons should be replicated in their dealings with their own free men and tenants. Earl Ranulf's charter was also destined, like the king's, to be repeatedly reissued or confirmed, so taking on a symbolic significance far beyond the immediate circumstances of its creation.

The factors which led to Cheshire becoming the only English county to have its 'own' Magna Carta are among the topics discussed in the pages which follow. There is also analysis of the meaning of the

---

[1] *Charters of the Anglo-Norman Earls of Chester, c.1071-1237*, ed. G. Barraclough (Record Society of Lancashire and Cheshire, CXXVI, 1988) [hereafter, *CEC*], no. 394, with discussion of the date on p. 392.

[2] 'Inquest of Military Service, 1288' in *Calendar of County Court, City Court and Eyre Rolls of Chester, 1259-1297*, ed. R. Stewart-Brown (Chetham Society, new series, LXXXIV, 1925), pp. 109, 113, where military service is to be done 'secundum proporttum magne communis carte Cestrisire', i.e. 'according to the tenor of the great common charter of Cheshire'. In both the Runnymede Magna Carta and its Cheshire counterpart, the clause numbers are those employed by historians for ease of reference, rather than original features. The numberings employed here follow Barraclough's edition of the charter and differ from those in *Chartulary or Register of St Werburgh, Chester*, ed. J. Tait (Chetham Society, new series, LXXIX, LXXXII, 1920, 1923), I, no. 60.

various clauses, alongside an English translation. We conclude with brief consideration of the subsequent history of the charter, and of its significance within the later administrative development of the county.

King John

> He was the very worst of all our kings ... to his people a hated tyrant. Polluted with every crime that could disgrace a man, false to every obligation that should bind a king ... he ... failed in every design he undertook ... In the whole view there is no redeeming trait; John seems as incapable of receiving a good impression as of carrying into effect a wise resolution.

So wrote one of the greatest of nineteenth-century medieval historians, William Stubbs - bishop of Chester from 1884 to 1889 - damning King John as an exceptionally 'bad king' in terms of both his personal behaviour and his governmental skills.[3] Most writers close in time to his reign testified to John's moral failings. One account, the *History of the Dukes of Normandy and Kings of England*, written a few years after John's death by an author in the entourage of one of his military commanders, described him as 'a very bad man, more cruel than all others [who] lusted after beautiful women and because of this he shamed the high men of the land, for which reason he was greatly hated'.[4]

The verdict of cruelty was based largely on the widespread belief that he had ordered the murders of several opponents, including his nephew (and rival claimant to the throne) Arthur of Brittany and

---

[3] W. Stubbs, *Constitutional History of England* (Oxford, 1896-97), II, p. 17, quoted in H.G. Richardson and G.O. Sayles, *The Governance of Mediaeval England from the Conquest to Magna Carta* (Edinburgh, 1963), p. 321.
[4] J. Gillingham, 'The Anonymous of Béthune, King John and Magna Carta' in J.S. Loengard, ed., *Magna Carta and the England of King John* (Woodbridge, 2010), pp. 27-44, with quotation on pp 37-38.

2

King John as he appears on his tomb in Worcester cathedral. (This is thought not to be a reliable likeness.)

members of the Braose family, former favourites against whom he had turned.[5] The accusation of lechery derived from outrage among his barons at the widely-known sexual harassment of their wives and daughters.[6] There was a grudging acknowledgement from Stubbs (in another part of the passage cited above) that John was 'not devoid of natural ability, craft or energy'; there is indeed plenty of evidence of his eagerness to travel his kingdom and of his active involvement in the business of government. But he often showed poor political

[5] For a reappraisal of the fall the Braose family, see C. Veach, 'King John and Royal Control in Ireland: Why William de Briouze had to be Destroyed', *English Historical Review* [hereafter *EHR*], CXXIX (2014), pp. 1051-78.
[6] J. Gillingham, 'John ... king of England ...' in *Oxford Dictionary of National Biography* (Oxford, 2004), XXX, pp. 158-70, esp. pp. 167-69.

judgment and his interventions tended to exacerbate rather than solve his problems. Mid-twentieth-century attempts to rehabilitate John as essentially an able ruler, unlucky and unfairly maligned,[7] have themselves been challenged and by the end of the century he was once again being seen as 'an unreliable and unpredictable king'. 'The fact that his subjects undertook forcibly to remove him from office must, in the end, be the lasting judgment on King John'.[8] No English monarch since has seen fit to revive the name.

This was the king whose political mistakes and misfortunes led to his humiliation at Runnymede in 1215. He succeeded in 1199 to an 'Angevin Empire' built by his father, Henry II, which encompassed not only the kingdom of England but the western half of France - Normandy, Brittany, Anjou, Maine, Touraine, Aquitaine including Poitou and Gascony - and extended to lordship of Scotland, Wales and Ireland as well.[9] In England itself, John also took over an efficient governmental system which had been refined over the last third of the twelfth century to make royal civil and criminal justice more accessible and taxes more lucrative, while enhancing the income from the king's customary perquisites as feudal overlord of his barons. However, John's reputation soon plummeted when, between 1202 and 1204, he lost all his continental lands except Gascony and the southernmost parts of Poitou to the resurgent king of France, Philip Augustus. The recovery of these lands, especially Normandy, became an enduring ambition for the rest of the reign, leading the king to exploit his opportunities to raise revenues to an unprecedented extent in the cause of financing the necessary campaigns - though it is fair to

---

[7] E.g. D. M. Stenton, *English Society in the Early Middle Ages* (London, 1951); W. L. Warren, *King John* (London, 1961); J. C. Holt, *King John* (Historical Association, 1963).
[8] J. Gillingham, 'Historians without Hindsight: Coggeshall, Diceto and Howden on the Early Years of John's Reign' and S.D. Church, 'Introduction' in S.D. Church, ed., *King John: New Interpretations* (Woodbridge, 1999), pp.1-26 (at p. 26) and pp. xix-xxvi (at p. xxvi).
[9] The term 'Angevin' derives from Henry II's paternal origins in Anjou.

add that selective financial extortion was also used as a means of exercising control through fear. Barons were liable to be charged excessive amounts on inheriting their lands (the payment known as relief), for the purchase of offices and for the king's interventions in their favour - to protect or promote their families' interests - and were then pressed hard for the debts, even to the point of being imprisoned or having their lands confiscated. Taxation and the profits of royal justice soared, especially after 1210, adding to perceptions of an oppressive regime. And there was no military success in France to justify the expense or to mollify those barons who had lost lands in Normandy or elsewhere and wanted them back; campaigns in 1206 and 1214 both ended in failure.

All this contributed to the widespread opinion among the baronage that John and his government were repugnant. The king followed many of the practices of his father Henry II and brother Richard I - especially the latter, whose extortions had been fuelled by price inflation and by the demands of his constant 'heroic' warfare, including his own ransom from captivity. But John's measures went well beyond the limits of what was considered reasonable and just. It did not help, either, that the king came increasingly to rely on French advisors who had come to England having lost their lands in 1202-04, so adding to the perception - not fully justified - that the well-established baronial families of the kingdom were being excluded from his counsels. The king's relationship with the papacy also contributed to an overall impression of weakness, although again the criticism was not entirely fair. In 1207, his refusal to accept Stephen Langton, Pope Innocent III's choice as archbishop of Canterbury - normally a post which went to the king's nominee - led to England being placed under an interdict, depriving his people of at least some of the sacraments, notably the mass and Christian burial. This was eventually lifted in 1214, after John had made reparations and - the previous year - acknowledged Langton and done homage to the pope as a vassal for his kingdom. Despite some comment, anticipating the Eurosceptics of today, to the effect that the country was being placed under a 'yoke of servitude',[10] this homage made no difference in practice to the king's authority and was actually an astute political move which notionally placed John under papal protection and wrong-footed his enemies. Far more significant than all this as an explanation of the background to Magna Carta was a range of personal grievances among a section of the baronage, mainly in the north and East Anglia, who felt that they had missed out on royal favour and patronage, and who could feed off widespread resentment of what was perceived as the king's repeated abuse of his powers. The consequence was conspiracy in 1212 and civil war three years later.

The path towards Runnymede can be tracked through a plot among a group of barons in summer 1212 - apparently to kill the king by one means or another - which led John to abandon a planned expedition to Wales and to demand hostages and the surrender of castles from those he suspected; through a refusal a year later, again on the part of northerners, to send knights for a projected invasion of Poitou, which had to be called off in consequence; through meetings between the king and baronial representatives late in 1213 at which he promised reforms he did not then deliver; through a refusal to pay scutage (a tax nominally in lieu of military service) on the part of barons over much of northern England and East Anglia to finance an expedition which did eventually reach Poitou in 1214; and through further negotiations between the king and baronial leaders, during the early months of 1215, with both parties forming themselves into armed camps. Ultimately, in May 1215, a group of rebel barons - still mostly from the north of England - formally renounced their fealty (sworn loyalty) to the king, led an army south and captured London: a move which seems to have persuaded the king that a settlement would have to be reached, even if only as a temporary expedient. That settlement was eventually concluded - as Magna Carta put it 'in the

---

[10] *Chronicle of Barnwell Priory*, quoted (as Walter of Coventry, who compiled it) in J.A.P. Jones, *King John and Magna Carta* (London, 1971), p. 42.

meadow that is called Runnymede between Windsor and Staines' - in the middle of June.[11]

Runnymede today, beside the River Thames with the road from Windsor to Staines passing through it.

The Earls of Chester

Although it has been reckoned that the number of leading figures who had never incurred the wrath of King John can be counted on one hand,[12] baronial opinion in 1215 was in fact fairly evenly divided between rebels and royalists, with a large third group which declined to commit to either side. It took a great deal of courage to take up arms against a king, whatever the provocation. This was one reason

---

[11] These episodes are recounted in all standard accounts of John's reign, but see, for example, J.C. Holt, *Magna Carta* (2nd edn., Cambridge, 1992), pp. 188-266. J.C. Holt, *The Northerners* (2nd edn., Oxford, 1992) is a justly-acclaimed study of the baronial movement.

[12] S. Painter, *The Reign of King John* (Baltimore, 1949), pp. 228-29.

why John felt sufficiently confident within a few weeks to renege on some of his promises and seek the pope's annulment of Magna Carta, so provoking the civil war which the charter had been designed to prevent. Among those who stayed loyal to the king in the crisis, despite friction between them in the past, was the man thought to have been at Richard I's death the wealthiest landholder in the country after John himself, Ranulf III (Ranulf de Blundeville) earl of Chester.[13] It is to his position, especially in relation to Cheshire, that we now turn.

Cheshire's boundaries had fluctuated, mainly to the north and west, since it had originated as an administrative unit probably in the early tenth century, but by the time Ranulf III became earl it encompassed an area broadly similar to that which prevailed until local government reorganisation in 1974. The significant exception - leaving aside minor nineteenth- and twentieth-century adjustments - was the territory between the Rivers Dee and Clwyd, treated as within Cheshire in Domesday Book but a disputed border zone which changed hands several times until the Edwardian conquest of the 1270s and 1280s.[14] A further issue is Cheshire's supposed 'palatine' status during the Middle Ages. In reality, the word is an unhelpful anachronism for the period before the 1290s, when it was first recorded in connection with the county. For the late-eleventh, twelfth and much of the thirteenth century, it is better not to join those who have worried about whether Cheshire fulfilled the supposed criteria

---

[13] Painter, *Reign of John*, p. 20; on John's suspicions about Earl Ranulf's disloyalty early in his reign, see I. Soden, *Ranulf de Blondeville: the First English Hero* (Stroud, 2009), pp. 34-49.
[14] *Victoria County History* [hereafter *VCH*]: *Cheshire*, I, (1987), p. 237; II (1979), pp. 94-95; N.J. Higham, *The Origins of Cheshire* (Manchester, 1993), pp. 1-3.

for a 'palatinate'[15] and simply examine what evidence we have of its governmental arrangements.[16]

We can begin by acknowledging that William the Conqueror had allowed his first earl of Chester, Hugh d'Avranches, to enjoy an unusually powerful position on the Welsh frontier, granting him lordship of every lay baron in Cheshire along with estates spread across a score of shires elsewhere in England. The motive was clearly to provide him with the authority and the resources both to defend the northern Welsh march and also to advance the Norman conquest into North Wales at the expense of Gwynedd and Powys. Earl Hugh had repaid the Conqueror's confidence in him by carrying the fight well beyond Cheshire's acknowledged boundaries into Anglesey and the Lleyn peninsula, earning a fearsome reputation in doing so, although by his death in 1101 the area under his control had effectively been pushed back to the River Conwy. The absence from Domesday Book of any royal demesne in Cheshire - land held directly by the crown - did not make the county unique, since in 1086 this was also true of neighbouring Shropshire. But it encouraged the earl to conceive of himself as occupying the king's place in Cheshire, with power to

---

[15] Notably by J.W. Alexander in 'New evidence on the Palatinate of Chester', *EHR*, LXXXV (1970), pp. 715-29 and *Ranulf of Chester, a Relic of the Conquest* (Athens, Georgia, 1983), esp. pp. 60-68.

[16] For what follows, see B. E. Harris, 'Ranulph III earl of Chester', *Journal of the Chester Archaeological Society*, LVIII (1975), pp. 99-114; *VCH: Cheshire*, II, pp. 1-6; A.T. Thacker, ed., *The Earldom of Chester and its Charters* (*Journal of Chester Archaeological Society*, LXXI, 1991), esp. within this A.T. Thacker, 'Introduction: the Earls and their Earldom', pp. 7-22, C.P. Lewis, 'The Formation of the Honor of Chester, 1066-1100', pp. 37-68 and D. Crouch, 'The Administration of the Norman Earldom', pp. 69-95; G.J. White, 'The Legacy of Ranulf de Gernons' in P. Dalton and D.E. Luscombe (eds.), *Rulership and Rebellion in the Anglo-Norman World, c.1066-c.1216: Essays in Honour of Professor Edmund King* (Farnham, 2015), pp. 111-24.

9

appoint his own sheriffs and to take revenues which would otherwise have gone to the king. In 1092-93, he founded a large Benedictine abbey at Chester which did not think it appropriate until several decades had passed to seek any royal confirmation.

Under Henry I, Cheshire's position became more anomalous still. By 1102, William the Conqueror's other marcher earldoms, based on Shropshire and Herefordshire, had both been forfeited to the crown following rebellion, allowing the former earls' lands to be redistributed. As for Wales, the king's preferred policy was now to reach an accommodation with the native rulers rather than to encourage the adventurism associated with Hugh d'Avranches. All this meant that the earls of Chester continued as lords of a county in which the king held no land, with substantial estates especially in Lincolnshire and the Midlands as well as in Cheshire, but were no longer expected to fulfil one of the original purposes of these arrangements, that of extending Norman control into Wales. In the pipe roll for 1129-30, detailing the accounts at the royal exchequer - the only one in an annual series to survive from Henry I's reign - Cheshire is one of a small number of counties missing altogether: a clear indication that the crown derived no income from the county, whether from land, from taxes or from the profits of the law courts.

By then, the earldom of Chester had passed to Ranulf II (Ranulf de Gernons), great-nephew of Hugh d'Avranches. He would achieve notoriety during the civil war of Stephen's reign (1135-54, although the war itself was a little shorter), fighting for both parties at different times in pursuit of further territorial aggrandizement and being described as one whose 'hand ... was against every man, and every man's hand against him'.[17] Since all the additional land he acquired during the war, at the expense of both the crown and of rival barons, was lost following his death in 1153, he tends to be written off as a deceitful and disruptive failure but there is some - admittedly

---

[17] *Gesta Stephani*, ed. K.R. Potter and R.H.C. Davis (Oxford, 1976), pp. 236-37, cf. pp. 198-99.

inconclusive - evidence that he initiated administrative reforms of long-term significance for the government of Cheshire. It is in Ranulf II's time that we first read of a 'justiciar of Chester' hearing judicial cases and of a 'chamber of Chester' dealing with the earl's finances, using processes not unlike those of the king's exchequer. Historians differ in their opinion of whether these arrangements covered the whole 'honour of Chester' - the complex of estates spread across the country - or only the county of Cheshire, but the evidence is consistent with both the justiciar and the chamber having a clear focus on the county from which Ranulf derived his earldom. If so, Cheshire was already being administered distinctively, separated out from the estates elsewhere in the country where the earl had other justiciars and financial offices and where the normal machinery of royal government was supposed to operate.

This remains unproven, but there are further signs of Cheshire's relative autonomy in the pipe rolls of Henry II's reign. Between 1158 and 1162, and again between 1181 and 1187, the Chester estates make a rare appearance in these rolls because of the minorities of the incumbent earls, first Ranulf II's son Hugh II (Hugh de Kyvelioc) and then Hugh II's son Ranulf III, when the income came to the king as guardian.[18] For some of these years, certainly between 1181 and 1185, Cheshire appears to have been accounted for separately, by a different local officer, from the rest of the honour. And for the period of Ranulf III's personal control of the earldom, from 1187 onwards, the evidence that Cheshire was perceived to be exceptional intensifies.

By 1202 at the latest, Ranulf III had appointed a chief justice or justiciar of Chester to preside over the county court on his behalf; his remit definitely focused on Cheshire rather than the remaining estates, and the earl went on to appoint to this post men drawn from the ranks of his leading landholders for the rest of his life. Probably by

---

[18] *Cheshire in the Pipe Rolls, 1158-1301*, ed. R. Stewart-Brown (Record Society of Lancashire and Cheshire, XCII, 1938), pp. 1-25.

1202 also, certainly by the end of the decade, a 'Domesday Roll of Cheshire' had been introduced, which in its enrolling of land grants and settlements seems to have been a local response to the practice introduced to the royal courts in the 1190s of keeping a record of agreements made before the king's justices.[19] A charter Ranulf issued concerning property in the city of Chester, sometime around 1210, reserved 'pleas of my sword' to be heard only before the earl or 'my chief justiciar', these 'pleas of my sword' evidently being seen as equivalent to the 'pleas of the crown' - the most serious criminal cases - reserved to the king or his justices in the rest of the country.[20] The earl also had a register of variously-worded writs, suitable for initiating different types of lawsuit in the Cheshire county court, to parallel the royal writs developed since the 1160s to begin actions before the king's justices; about 1220, for example, he issued a writ of *mort d'ancestor* - presumably modelled on similar writs introduced by Henry II - to begin a suit over land in Budworth, involving two members of the Grosvenor family.[21] It is clear, also, that by the 1230s - when the death without issue first of Ranulf III then of his nephew John le Scot allowed lordship of Cheshire to pass to the crown and caused the honour to be fragmented among various claimants - a separate financial office for the county had become well-established. This was recognisable to the royal officials who took it over as an 'exchequer', with procedures similar to those of the king's, and it was permitted to continue to handle the county's financial accounts

---

[19] R. Stewart-Brown, 'The Domesday Roll of Cheshire', *EHR*, XXXVII (1922), pp. 481-500, esp. pp. 493-500; G. Barraclough, 'The Earldom and County Palatine of Chester', *Transactions of the Historic Society of Lancashire and Cheshire*, CIII (1951), pp. 23-57, at pp. 35-36.

[20] *CEC*, no. 282; on the equivalence of 'pleas of the sword' to 'pleas of the crown', see e.g. F. Pollock and F.W. Maitland, *The History of English Law* (2nd edn., reissued, Cambridge, 1968), II, pp. 453-56.

[21] *CEC*, no. 397 (not the writ itself but a subsequent intervention which refers back to it); Barraclough, 'Earldom and County Palatine', p. 35. The writ of *mort d'ancestor* was intended to provide speedy redress for an heir who was being denied possession of his dead forebear's land.

thereafter, albeit now on behalf of the crown rather than of the local earl.

In all this, a degree of administrative independence, much of the detail of which is lost, intermingled with perceptions of separatism, deliberately fostered by successive earls and their barons. As governmental reforms progressively strengthened royal control of the kingdom in the second half of the twelfth century, so the county came to appear more isolated, beyond the reach of the king's officials except in relation to the bishopric of Chester (otherwise Coventry and Lichfield), an institution about which the king continued to give the earl instructions.[22] None of the taxes Henry II imposed with some frequency on the rest of the country - such as scutage and levies on landholders variously described as *auxilia* (aids) and *dona* (gifts) - seem to have been collected from the county. In 1166, when the king ordered an enquiry through his sheriffs into the number and names of knights who owed military service - resulting in the so-called *Cartae Baronum* returned by those who held their estates directly from him - Cheshire was omitted altogether from the survey. None of Henry II's itinerant justices appear to have crossed into Cheshire armed with the new judicial procedures - the various 'possessory assizes' introduced in the 1160s and 1170s - which offered speedy redress and brought greater consistency to judicial process (a 'common law'), increased the business of the royal courts and generated more income for the crown as a result.[23] This is the obvious conclusion to be drawn from Cheshire's routine absence from the pipe rolls and even during the few years when it did appear, during the minorities of earls Hugh II and Ranulf III, there is no reference to any revenue generated for the

---

[22] Harris, 'Ranulph III', p. 110; *VCH: Cheshire*, II, p. 6.
[23] On this, see e.g. W.L. Warren, *The Governance of Norman and Angevin England, 1086-1272* (London, 1987), pp. 105-22; J. Hudson, *The Formation of the English Common Law* (London, 1996), pp. 118-219; J. Hudson, *The Oxford History of the Laws of England, II, 817-1216* (Oxford, 2012), esp. pp. 497-536.

crown from taxation or from the implementation of new judicial procedures.

There were in fact several enclaves within late-twelfth-century England where, in one or more respects, 'normal' royal government did not operate in full: Cornwall, Durham, the Isle of Wight among them.[24] In Cheshire, however, autonomy was compounded by the fact that control rested with one of the wealthiest baronial families in the kingdom. As we have seen, Ranulf III was a minor under the wardship of Henry II for six years from 1181, but far from having his position as earl of Chester curtailed he found himself being married (probably in 1188) to the widow of the king's late brother Geoffrey: a brilliant match which made Ranulf duke of Brittany and earl of Richmond in right of his wife, so adding further grand titles as well as estates. The result was that by the end of Richard I's reign in April 1199 the earldom of Chester was in the hands of a great baron whose outstanding wealth embraced estates stretching from coast to coast across the Midlands and north of England, as well as on Normandy's western flank; a man whose wife brought him a ducal title in Brittany to match those held by the king in Normandy and Aquitaine (although Ranulf would lose this through the termination of his marriage within months of John's accession); and one who governed a county on the northern Welsh border with scarcely any intervention from the king or his officials.

Ranulf III was certainly considered within Cheshire to enjoy an exceptional degree of authority. In 1194, according to the Chester abbey chronicle, the 'glorious earl' secured the removal of an unpopular abbot nominated by the king during Ranulf's minority.[25] It was also around that time that the Chester monk Lucian described Ranulf as a prince ('princeps'), not a formal title used in his charters but one traditionally associated with rulership of a distinct people, like

---

[24] See, for example, Hudson, *Oxford History of the Laws*, pp. 562-65.
[25] *Annales Cestrienses*, ed. R.C. Christie (Record Society of Lancashire and Cheshire, XIV, 1887), pp. 34-35, 44-45.

those of Bavaria, Burgundy or Wales. 'Both by royal permission', he wrote, 'and the virtues of its earls', Cheshire 'is accustomed to answer in its assemblies more to the sword of its prince than the crown of the king'.[26] Although there was to be nothing in Magna Carta specifically excluding Cheshire from its provisions, there was evidently a sufficiently-strong sense of independence among the county's politically-aware elite to make the issue of a separate document a feasible proposition.

The Runnymede Magna Carta[27]

There is no single definitive copy of King John's Magna Carta. It survives in four virtually-identical versions, two of which are now in Lincoln and Salisbury cathedrals, the other two in the British Library. They must be regarded as only a sample of those originally distributed, to be read out in the shire courts, but there is no evidence that a copy was ever received in Cheshire. In most cases the copies were not committed to safe-keeping since they were quickly superseded by the various reissues to which we shall turn later on. The king definitely did not sign anything; nor did he personally append his seal to any of the copies for distribution, since this was a task for one of his chancery officials, the spigurnel. Essentially, Magna Carta must

---

[26] *Liber Luciani de Laude Cestrie*, ed. M.V. Taylor (Record Society of Lancashire and Cheshire, LXIV, 1912), p. 65; Crouch, 'Administration', pp. 71-72.

[27] This section largely follows J.C. Holt, *Magna Carta* (2nd edn., Cambridge, 1992), pp. 242-66, 441-73, and also pp. 494-95 where Cheshire is omitted from a list of counties for which copies of Magna Carta sent out in late June and July 1215 were intended. There is also an excellent summary of the context, content and subsequent influence of Magna Carta in N. Vincent, *Magna Carta: A Very Short Introduction* (Oxford, 2012). Holt (on pp. 248-59) and Vincent (on p. 72) differ on their interpretation of the significance of the date of 15 June which appears in Magna Carta. Among the many relevant publications marking the 800th anniversary, attention is drawn in particular to D. A. Carpenter, *Magna Carta* (London, 2015) and N. Vincent, *Magna Carta: Making and Legacy* (Oxford, 2015).

be seen as a record of the settlement agreed at Runnymede in the days following 10 June, when John apparently arrived on the meadow. It states that it was 'given by our hand' on 15 June following oaths taken by both parties to observe its terms 'in good faith and without evil intent'; this was evidently the date when the parties reached fundamental agreement, and may have been that when the first copy was sealed, but in any event many more copies were to follow over the next few weeks. Related documents, including so-called 'Articles of the Barons' which rehearse nearly all the clauses of Magna Carta but in draft form, represent stages in the negotiations, during which Archbishop Langton may have played a critical role as mediator.

Many of the clauses of Magna Carta dealt squarely with the grievances barons felt about the way John had abused the conventions of Angevin royal government. These were mostly in the early part of the document: seeking to limit the amount which could be charged as relief (clauses 2, 43), to curb exploitation of estates by their temporary custodians (3-5, 43), to protect the interests of heirs and widows in matters of marriage (6-8), to limit the penalties which could be incurred through unpaid debts (9-11, 26) and to restrict the king's freedom to levy taxes (scutages and aids) except with the consent of 'the common counsel of the kingdom', defined as the greater clergy and barons along with all who held of the king direct (12, 14, 15). There were a number, also, which dealt with the conduct of justice (17-22, 24, 34, 36, 38-40, 44, 45, 52, 54-57), intent for the most part not to challenge the reach of the royal law-courts but to enhance their fairness, efficiency and accessibility. Beyond all this, grievances surfaced over restrictions associated with royal forests (47, 48) and there were clauses safeguarding the liberties of London and other towns (13), the navigation of rivers (33) and the movement of merchants and other travellers (41, 42). Some clauses made statements in the grandest terms: 'the English church shall be free' (1, 63) and 'to no one shall we sell, to no one shall we refuse or delay right or justice' (40). Others were concerned with immediate practicalities, such as the return of hostages (49, 58, 59), the removal of John's foreign

16

mercenaries from the kingdom (50, 51) and an amnesty for offences committed as part of the present 'quarrel' (62). The famous 'security clause' (61) provided for 25 barons to be elected by their peers, with powers to coerce the king if he transgressed the terms agreed. Clause 60, emphasising what had already been implicit elsewhere in the charter, ensured that the concessions would benefit others besides those who enjoyed an immediate relationship with the king:

> All these aforesaid customs and liberties which we have granted to be held in our realm as far as pertains to us towards our men will be observed by all men of our realm, both clerks and laymen, as far as pertains to them towards their own men.[28]

There were in fact precedents for this instruction to the barons to 'do as they would be done by' as far back as Henry I's coronation charter of 1100.[29] However, this was one of the clauses which in the long term would give Magna Carta its mythical status as a grant of liberties to the people of England as a whole. The parallels between this clause and clause 13 of Ranulf III's great charter point strongly to the conclusion that those who framed the Cheshire document were familiar with that issued at Runnymede.

Earl Ranulf's Magna Carta

The Magna Carta of Cheshire is readily available in print in Ormerod's nineteenth-century *History*, in Tait's edition of the Chester abbey cartulary (1920), and in Barraclough's collection of the earldom of Chester charters (1988). Unlike John's Magna Carta, no contemporary version survives, although since the seventeenth-century Cheshire antiquarian Randle Holme claimed to have had two sealed originals in front of him as he made a copy from them, it is not

---

[28] The translation of this clause, and of those below, follows Vincent, *Magna Carta*, pp. 111-24.
[29] *English Historical Documents* [hereafter *EHD*], II, no. 19 (caps. 2, 4).

17

impossible that one will turn up! As Barraclough points out, Holme's statement - for what it is worth - implies that, as at Runnymede, several exemplifications of the charter were sealed and distributed, rather than there being a single definitive original.[30]

The earliest manuscript version of the charter, an illustration of which appears below, is an enrolled copy of a confirmation by Edward I, dating to 1300. This is an *inspeximus*, opening with an explanation that the king has inspected the relevant document and then proceeding to quote it in full. It is accompanied at the end by a reference to a previous confirmation by Edward, who had received Cheshire in 1254; this earlier document, which does not survive independently, was dated 1265, prior to his accession as king.[31] Conceivably, there is cause for concern here. In the years following the crown's takeover of the county in the 1230s, might the Cheshire barons have embellished Ranulf's concessions in their own interests, presenting an 'improved' version of some of the clauses for confirmation in 1265 or 1300? Fortunately, this possibility can be dismissed. On the one hand, we also have Holme's transcribed copy of the charter, based as he explained on two of Ranulf's sealed originals.[32] Obviously it is not ideal to have to depend on a seventeenth-century transcription but Holme's version and Edward I's confirmation are virtually identical. Both are later copies of the document issued by Earl Ranulf but their provenance is different and in the absence of any discrepancy between them - other than some minor variations in spelling - they serve to verify one another's accuracy. Beyond this, the reference in the 1300 enrolment to the confirmation of Ranulf's charter in 1265 indicates that the Cheshire barons did indeed obtain some extra concessions on that occasion, but

---

[30] *CEC*, p. 392.
[31] The National Archives, C66/120, m. 22.
[32] British Library, Harl. MS 2071, f. 18v.

18

these are clearly set out as additions which were not to be regarded, then or in the future, as part of the charter.[33]

Holme's copy was that favoured by Barraclough for his edition of the charter and Barraclough's text, in turn, is the one relied upon here, both for the translation by Jonathan Pepler which follows and for the Latin version which appears in the Appendix. Any reader interested in the tiny textual variants between different copies of the charter may refer to the annotations provided by Barraclough. This is not the first publication of the document in English, since translations have appeared previously, both in Hemingway's *History of the City of Chester* in 1831 and in Ormerod; there is also a detailed abstract of its contents in a volume of the *Calendar of Patent Rolls* dating to 1895.[34] However, it is the first full translation to be based on a rendering of the Latin text to modern standards of scholarship. Even in a translation there are several terms which are unfamiliar to a modern reader, but these will be explained in the accompanying commentary.

---

[33] The additional concessions in 1265 granted the lord of a convicted Cheshire felon entitlement to his forfeited lands after a year and a day and made clear that recent military service to Edward outside the county was not to be treated as a precedent. On this see J. R. Studd, 'The Lord Edward's Lordship of Chester, 1254-72', *Transactions of the Historic Society of Lancashire and Cheshire*, CXXVIII (1979), pp. 1-25, at p. 16.

[34] G. Ormerod, *History of the County Palatine and City of Chester* (rev. edn. by T. Helsby, London, 1882), I, pp. 53-55; *Chartulary of St Werburgh, Chester*, ed. Tait, I, no. 60, with discussion on pp. 101-102, 107-109; J. Hemingway, *History of the City of Chester* (Chester, 1831), I, pp. 121-23; also (for Barraclough), note 1 above. Tait did not reproduce the cartulary text as it stood because it contained abbreviations, preferring the fuller version of 1300 in the Public Record Office (now The National Archives), an image of which is published here. This is also the version of which an abstract appears in *Calendar of Patent Rolls, Edward I, 1292-1301* (HMSO, London, 1895), pp. 499-500.

Ranulf Earl of Chester, to the constable, steward, justiciar, sheriff, barons and bailiffs and all his men and friends, both present and future, who will see or hear this present charter, greeting. Know that I, being signed with the cross, have, for the love of God and at the petition of my barons of Cheshire, granted to them and their heirs, from me and my heirs, all the liberties written hereunder in this present charter, to be held and had in perpetuity, namely:

1. *That each one of them may have his own court free from all pleas and complaints being moved in my court, except pleas pertaining to my sword, and that if any one of his men shall be taken for any offence, throughout his lordship, he may be reclaimed without ransom, so that his lord may bring him to three county [courts], and may take him back acquitted, unless a sacraber pursues him.*

2. *And if a stranger, who is trustworthy, should come into their lands and wishes to stay there, it may be lawful for the baron to have and keep him, saving to me those avowers who may come to me of their own accord and others who on account of transgressions committed elsewhere may come to my dignity, and not to them.*

3. *And each one of the barons, when need may require in war, shall fully perform the service of as many knights' fees as he holds, and their knights and free tenants shall have breastplates and haubergeons, and may defend their fees with their own bodies, even if they are not knights. And if there be any one of them such that he cannot defend his land with his own body, he may put another sufficient person in his place. Nor shall I make their villeins swear to arms, but I*

20

grant to them quit their villeins who came to my avowry through Ranulf de Davenham, and their other villeins whom they may reasonably show to be theirs.

4. *And if my sheriff or any serjeant in my court shall have accused any one of their men, he may defend himself by 'thwertnic' on account of the 'sirevestoth' which they pay, unless the suit pursues him.*

5. *And I grant them quittance of sheaves and offerings which my serjeants and beadles were accustomed to demand. And that if any judge or suitor of the hundred or county should incur amercement in my court, a judge may be quit of the amercement for two shillings and a suitor for twelve pence.*

6. *And I grant them liberty of assarting their lands within the bounds of their husbandry in the forest, and if there should be land or territory within the bounds of their vills, which was formerly cultivated, and wood does not grow there, they may cultivate it without harbourage, and they may take 'husbote' and 'haybote' in their wood of all sorts of timber without view of the forester, and they may give or sell dead wood to whomever they wish. And their men may not be impleaded concerning the forest for the above mentioned, unless they are caught red-handed.*

7. *And each one of them may defend all his demesne manors in the county [court] and hundred [court] by one steward there present.*

8. *And I grant that, when a man dies, his wife may peacefully occupy his house for forty days. And his heir, if he is of age,*

may have his inheritance for a reasonable relief, namely a hundred shillings for a knight's fee. Neither the lady nor the heir shall be married where this would involve loss of rank, but by the favour and assent of their family. And their legacies shall be secured.

9. *And none of them may lose his villein in the event of him coming into the city of Chester, unless he stays there for a year and a day without challenge.*

10. *And on account of the heavy service which they perform in Cheshire, none of them shall do service for me beyond the Lyme, unless of their own free will and at my expense. And if my knights from England who owe me ward at Chester are summoned, and have come to perform their ward, and the army of my enemies from elsewhere is not present, and there is no necessity, my barons may meanwhile freely return to their homes and rest. And if an army of my enemies should be prepared to come into my land in Cheshire, or if the castle should be besieged, the aforesaid barons will come immediately at my summons with their army and exertions, to remove that army as far as they are able. And when that army shall have retreated from my land, the said barons can return to their lands with their army, and rest, while the knights from England perform their ward and there shall be no necessity for them, save for the services which they must do for me.*

11. *And I grant to them that in time of peace only twelve itinerant serjeants may be kept in my land with one horse which is for the master serjeant, and which may not have provender from Easter until the feast of Saint Michael,*

except voluntarily; and that those same serjeants may eat such food as they may find in men's houses, without the purchase of other food for their use, nor may they eat in any of the barons' demesnes. And in time of war, on my advice or that of my justiciar and themselves [the barons], sufficient serjeants may be put in place to guard my land as the need may be.

12. *And may it be known that the aforesaid barons have completely remitted to me and my heirs, on behalf of themselves and their heirs, the following petitions which they were asking from me, so that they can claim nothing in relation to them henceforth, unless by my grace and mercy: namely, the steward his petition for wreck and fish washed up on his land by the sea, and for shooting in my forest with three bows, and for hunting with his dogs; and others the petition for the agistment of pigs in my forest and for shooting with three bows in my forest, or for the coursing of their hares in the forest on the way to, or returning from Chester in response to a summons; and the petition for the amercement of the judges of Wich thirty boilings of salt, but the amercement and laws in Wich shall be as they were before.*

13. *I grant therefore, and by this my present charter confirm, for me and my heirs, to all common knights and free tenants of the whole of Cheshire and their heirs, all the aforesaid liberties, to be had and held of my barons and of their other lords, whoever they may be, just as the barons and knights themselves and other free tenants hold them of me.*

These being witnesses: Hugh Abbot of Saint Werburgh Chester, Philip de Orreby at that time justiciar of Chester, Henry de Aldithlega [Audley], Walter Deyville, Hugh the dispenser, Thomas the dispenser, William the butler, Walter de Coventry, Richard Phitun, Robert de Coudrey, Ivo de Kaletoft, Robert de Say, Norman de Paunton, Robert the dispenser, Robert Deyville, Matthew de Vernun [Vernon], Hamo de Venables, Robert de Masci, Alan de Waley, Hugh de Culumbe, Robert de Pulfort [Pulford], Peter the clerk, Hugh de Pasci, Joceram de Helesby [Helsby], Richard de Bresci, Richard de Kingesle [Kingsley], Philip de Therven, Lithulf de Thwamlawe [Twemlow], Richard de Perpunt and the whole county [court] of Chester.

Commentary on the Cheshire Magna Carta

Date and Context

Since the charter mentions that Earl Ranulf was 'signed with the cross' - that is, had vowed to go on crusade - it must have been issued sometime after Ash Wednesday (4 March) 1215, when he is known to have joined King John in making this commitment.[35] It cannot be later than 19 October 1216, when John died, since the Chester abbey chronicle notes the death of one of the witnesses, Hugh de Pascy, as a previous event.[36] Within this period, Ranulf - who had fought for the king on the unsuccessful campaign in Poitou in 1214 and had helped to negotiate the eventual truce - was often in John's company during the tense early months of 1215, although there is no sign of his presence at Runnymede. He was not among the 'noble men' listed in Magna Carta as those on whose advice the king acted, such as William Marshal earl of Pembroke and William earl of Salisbury. He

---

[35] Gervase of Canterbury, *Opera Historica*, ed. W. Stubbs (Rolls Series, 1879-80), II, p. 109.
[36] *Annales Cestrienses*, ed. Christie, pp. 50-51. Names such as Pasci and Masci in the charter have been rendered in the commentary as ending in -y.

was present with John, however, at a council held at Oxford just after the middle of July, when business left unresolved at Runnymede was supposed to have been settled and when continued acrimony is thought finally to have convinced the king that Magna Carta should be annulled.[37]

---

[37] Holt, *Magna Carta*, pp. 365-67, 484-89.

Previous page: The block of text in the top half of the image is the earliest extant copy of the 'Cheshire Magna Carta', as it appears on a Chancery Patent Roll. This records Edward I's confirmation (dated 30 March 1300) of Earl Ranulf III's charter, repeating the text and referring to an earlier confirmation by Edward of 27 August 1265, when he held Cheshire but was not yet king. (The National Archives, ref. C66/120 m. 22, reproduced by permission.)

Thereafter, once civil war had broken out in September, with the rebels soon offering the crown to the future Louis VIII, heir to the French throne, Ranulf's support was to be crucial to John.[38] Apart from helping to keep the Welsh borders loyal, he was an active campaigner as a leading royalist military commander, forcing the surrender of castles in Yorkshire early in 1216, for example, and seizing Worcester that summer after it had declared for Louis following the French invasion in May. His value to the king at this time is apparent from the further grants of lands and offices he received, including the holdings of rebel barons in the Midlands as an incentive to attack them. And after John's death from dysentery in autumn 1216 had unexpectedly transformed the political situation - depriving the rebels of the main focus of their grievances - Ranulf would go on (as we shall see) to play a key role in pacifying the kingdom and securing recognition for the young heir Henry III. For this he would receive yet more reward in the form of the earldom of Lincoln in May 1217.

All this makes the weeks between the Runnymede settlement in mid-June 1215 and the outbreak of civil war that autumn the most likely period for the issue of Earl Ranulf's charter. Nearly all historians consider King John's document to be the earlier of the two;

---

[38] On all this, see, for example, Painter, *Reign of John*, pp. 349-77; Soden, *Ranulf de Blondeville*, pp. 65-80; R. Eales, 'Ranulf [III] sixth earl of Chester ...'in *Oxford Dictionary of National Biography*, XLVI, pp. 56-59.

given the similarity of some of the clauses this is surely correct.[39] And for the duration of the civil war, Ranulf was rarely in Cheshire with time to meet his barons in the county court. As for whatever negotiations preceded the grant of the charter, we know from the opening section and from clause 12 that it was based on petitions presented by the Cheshire barons and that the earl rejected some of their proposals. Barraclough suggested that Ranulf's taking of the cross in early March - so bringing him under the protection of the Church which would now condemn those who harassed him over matters in dispute - was a sign that he was already 'anticipating trouble'; he also thought that the Cheshire barons may have been formulating their petitions early in 1215, at the same time as John's opponents were conducting preliminary - initially fruitless - negotiations with the king.[40] However, this can be no more than hypothesis. An alternative is that the spectacle of copies of Magna Carta being sent for reading in every other county of England during late June and July - to the accompaniment of local inquests into abuses committed by the king's officers, as provided for in clause 48[41] - led the barons of Cheshire to petition for a charter of their own. If so - allowing time for some hard bargaining - the Cheshire document can hardly be much earlier than the end of July 2015 and may well belong

---

[39] On the Cheshire Magna Carta post-dating that issued at Runnymede, see e.g. *Chartulary of St Werburgh, Chester*, ed. Tait, I, p. 107 and Barraclough in *CEC*, p. 392. See also the commentary on clause 13, below. A contrary view was expressed by Brian Harris, who in an excellent paper to the Chester Archaeological Society in 1971 entertained the possibility that the Cheshire Magna Carta ('which deserves more study than it has so far received') might have come first ('Ranulph III', p. 112). However, such similarities as there are between the two documents would, on this scenario, imply a role for the Cheshire charter in influencing the Runnymede text, with Earl Ranulf or an associate presumably helping to draft it, and there is no evidence for this whatsoever.
[40] *CEC*, p. 392.
[41] Cf. Holt, *Magna Carta*, pp. 340, 352-54, 384-85, 494-95.

27

to late August or September, as Ranulf sought to ensure his barons' loyalty in preparation for the inevitable conflict ahead.

Parallels between King John's Magna Carta and that issued for Cheshire must not be stretched too far. However sceptical historians may be about some modern reconstructions of the scene at Runnymede, an image of a tense, crowded and colourful meadow, bustling with the armed retinues of the king and of a throng of barons with accompanying clergy, is not far off the mark. The granting of the Cheshire charter was a more subdued affair. There is no hint of any armed confrontation and the barons who evidently negotiated its terms - or at least led the negotiations, perhaps in company with others - could be counted on the fingers of two hands. The term 'baron' is an elastic one, usually employed today (and in the early thirteenth century) to designate the greater landholders among the tenants-in-chief - that is, tenants holding directly of the king. In twelfth-century Cheshire, however, it was a title enjoyed by the holders of eight estates, each named after its administrative centre: Dunham (Massey), Halton, Kinderton, Malpas, Mold, Nantwich, Shipbrook and Stockport. By the early thirteenth century, two of these (Malpas and Nantwich) had fragmented and, to judge from the attestations to Ranulf III's charters, the politically-active Cheshire barons by 1215 were those of Dunham (Hamo de Mascy), Halton (the earl's hereditary constable, John de Lacy), Kinderton (William de Venables), Mold (the earl's hereditary steward, Roger de Montalt) and Shipbrook (Warin de Vernon, who had also taken a share of Nantwich). It is of course quite possible that they were joined in their negotiations with the earl by other prominent landholders such as Roger de Mainwaring, lord of Warmingham near Sandbach, and Robert Patrick who by now had a share in the barony of Malpas. But none of the baronies comprised more than ten knights' fees held of the earl in Cheshire - estates from which the military service of ten knights was due - compared to the substantial double or even triple-digit holdings among those who composed the 'Twenty-Five' leaders of the opposition to King John.[42]

The Cheshire barons were not, however, isolated from the affairs of the rest of the kingdom, since Hugh d'Avranches had arranged for their ancestors to receive estates within the honour of Chester elsewhere in England, as well as in Cheshire itself.[43] In particular, one of their number, John de Lacy the 'baron of Halton', was also a major tenant-in-chief of the king, especially in Yorkshire and Lancashire; de Lacy had his own grievances against royal government owing to the exorbitant sum he had been obliged to pay to take possession of these inherited estates, far more extensive than those he held in Cheshire. He was present at Runnymede and was included among the 'Twenty-Five' charged with ensuring that Magna Carta was observed. We cannot know, but if there is one man who might have led the demands for a local equivalent in Cheshire, John de Lacy is an obvious candidate. That said, if we are right to see the issue of this charter as prompted by a need to secure baronial loyalties ahead of the forthcoming conflict, it failed in the case of de Lacy, who (as a man with much more at stake outside the county) fought on the opposite side to Earl Ranulf for much of the ensuing civil war.[44]

It is tempting to suggest that Ranulf III positively welcomed the opportunity to issue his great charter, as a demonstration of his standing in Cheshire in place of the king. That would be a mistake. First, while John was still alive, Magna Carta was seen by his friends

---

[42] *Calendar of Court Rolls of Chester*, ed. Stewart-Brown, pp. xlvi-xlvii; *VCH: Cheshire*, I, pp. 306-14.

[43] Lewis, 'Formation', pp. 59-61.

[44]   <<http://www.magnacartabarons.info/index.php/the-barons/lacy-john-de/>>, accessed 29/7/14; Holt, *The Northerners*, pp. 1, 26. Despite submitting to King John at the beginning of 1216, John de Lacy had rejoined the rebels by the time of the king's death in October, so featuring on the opposite side to Earl Ranulf.

and foes alike as a humiliating constraint on the king's authority, extorted from him by the threat of force: not an image which Earl Ranulf would willingly have projected onto Cheshire. Secondly, there would be several future opportunities for the earl to reissue or formally confirm the Cheshire charter, to accompany the various reissues of Magna Carta in 1216, 1217 and 1225 - occasions intended to enhance rather than to challenge the authority of the next king Henry III, as discussed below - but he chose not to do so. Yet if Ranulf granted concessions to his Cheshire barons reluctantly, there was nevertheless some political capital to be gained from the exercise. The experience of the earl presiding over the county court, in order to make grants some of which were clearly modelled on those in Magna Carta, was striking testimony to a self-conscious sense of Cheshire's independence from the rest of the kingdom. And the charter was carefully worded to minimise the impression that Ranulf's power over the county was in any way diminished. Indeed, several of the clauses, including the first three, specifically affirmed the earl's rights as well as those of his barons.

In this connection, it is worth asking what we can reasonably infer from the various clauses about Ranulf III's regime in Cheshire. Given the circumstances in which the Runnymede Magna Carta was produced, the fact that there is a clause dealing with a particular issue repeatedly leads to the conclusion that the king must have been abusing his powers in this area. With the Cheshire Magna Carta, we cannot make an equivalent assumption. Occasionally, there is a pointed reference to a named individual (clause 3) or we are specifically told that there would be a change of practice (clause 5); in these cases, particular grievances must lie behind the statements. Wherever the earl's officials are mentioned (as in clause 11), we may suspect that they had been over-reaching themselves and were having to be reined in. But much of the charter, especially where it is concerned with the maintenance of distinctive Cheshire customs, may simply have been an expression of the barons' wish to secure a guarantee of their privileges by having them written down. We should not assume without further evidence that the earl had been causing serious offence. This is a matter dealt with more fully in the commentaries on the individual clauses which follow.

Introductory section

There had been no attempt in the introduction to King John's Magna Carta to disguise the exceptional nature of the document. Though addressed, as was customary, to the ecclesiastical and lay baronage, several royal officials and all faithful subjects, it had made clear that it was being issued 'for the reform of our realm' and on the advice of a long list of senior clergy and loyal barons identified by name. Earl Ranulf's charter, on the other hand, seems deliberately to have been drafted to read as normally as possible, giving little hint of any pressure which he might have been under to grant the various concessions. The opening greeting to his barons, men and various administrative officers used phraseology familiar from several of his other charters, mostly dealing with small grants of property. And although the opening section does acknowledge that the concessions were being made 'at the petition of my barons of Cheshire' this was countered by the later statement, in clause 12, that they themselves had 'remitted' some of their demands; in other words, the earl had turned them down. This was a charter intended to leave his authority intact.

'For the avoidance of doubt', as modern lawyers are fond of saying, it is worth adding that this introductory section, along with several of the clauses and the concluding reference among the witnesses to 'all the county of Chester', make it abundantly clear that the charter was intended to apply only within Cheshire itself, the shire from which Ranulf derived his earldom. The concessions did not extend to the earl's vast honour elsewhere in England. The one reference to it, in clause 10, concerned duties owed generally in relation to the castle at Chester.

31

Clause 1

The very first issue to be addressed was that of the respective powers of the earl's and barons' courts. As we have seen, the last third of the twelfth century had witnessed several reforms which had increased the scope and activity of the royal courts, with most of the relevant clauses in the Runnymede Magna Carta accepting this development in principle but requiring amendment in practice. Only one of them, no. 34, had implied any resentment at the loss of jurisdiction by lesser court-holders:

> The writ called *praecipe* will not in future be issued to anyone in respect of any holding whereby a free man might lose his court.

The concern here had been that the royal writ *praecipe* ('command') was being used to remove cases to the king's court which would otherwise have come before a baronial court; even in this instance, modern interpretations - citing an established process whereby a baron could 'reclaim his court' - suggest that only a modest sense of grievance at what Holt calls 'an administrative nuisance' lay behind it.[45] For our purposes, however, the key point is that these various advances in judicial procedure before the king or his justices had not penetrated Cheshire; if the Cheshire barons had encountered them, they had done so only in respect of their holdings elsewhere in the kingdom. It was all the more important, therefore, that in the absence of 'royal justice' they were satisfied with the workings of the earl of

---

[45] N.D. Hurnard, 'Magna Carta, Clause 34' in R.W. Hunt, W.A. Pantin and R.W. Southern, eds., *Studies in Medieval History presented to F.M. Powicke* (Oxford, 1948), pp. 157-79; M.T. Clanchy, 'Magna Carta, Clause Thirty-Four', *EHR,* LXXIX (1964), pp. 542-47; Hudson, *Formation,* p. 225; Hudson, *Oxford History of the Laws,* pp. 559-60; *The Treatise on the Laws and Customs of the Realm, of England commonly called Glanvill,* ed. G.D.G. Hall (London, 1965), p. 5; Holt, *Magna Carta,* pp. 325-26 (quotation on p. 326).

Chester's court, and it may be no accident that this was the first subject dealt with in the charter.

The opening part of this clause makes it clear that the full range of judicial business, civil and criminal, was in focus, although there was no challenge to the earl's jurisdiction over the most serious criminal cases (the 'pleas pertaining to my sword'). As we have seen, these 'pleas of the sword' were the earl's local equivalent of 'pleas of the crown' elsewhere. As such they would have embraced homicide, arson, rape, robbery with violence and also thefts of a nature or scale to merit the penalty of death or mutilation. For their part, the Cheshire barons, like major landholders all over the country, had a customary entitlement to hear and settle civil suits involving their own tenants and also enjoyed rights of criminal jurisdiction over lesser offences such as woundings, unruly behaviour and in some circumstances also theft: either because the criminal belonged to one's estate and was caught red-handed in possession of stolen goods or (it seems) if only small items or sums were involved.[46]

---

[46] On all this, see e.g. Pollock and Maitland, *History of English Law*, I, pp. 568-82, Hudson, *Formation*, pp. 40-47, 160-66, 175; Hudson, *Oxford History of the Laws*, pp. 289-91, 562. *Glanvill*, ed. Hall, pp. 3-4, 177, lists 'brawlings, beatings and ... wounding' among the offences which could be dealt with by lords because they were not crown pleas and includes theft among them as well; however - as noted, for example, by Hall at p. 177 n. 1 - theft was sometimes regarded as a crown plea and some distinction based on value or context seems most likely. Jurisdiction over the 'red-handed' thief was covered by the right known as 'infangentheof', entitlement to hang such a person after a summary trial if (s)he dwelt on one's estate and was caught within its bounds. A less usual privilege was that of 'outfangentheof', the right to hang a thief from one's estate wherever (s)he was caught 'red-handed'. Privileges claimed by Sir Hamo de Mascy of Dunham apparently in the early fourteenth century - supposedly enjoyed since time immemorial - included both 'infangentheof' and 'outfangentheof' (Ormerod, *History of the County Palatine*, 1882, I, p. 526) and this probably applied to all the Cheshire barons.

33

It is impossible to be sure how far the Cheshire barons, in demanding this concession, actually felt their established judicial authority to be under threat. There may have been some resentment at Earl Ranulf's practice of granting to a privileged few the right to answer in any judicial dispute only before the earl or his chief justice.[47] His issue of writs modelled on those of the king, like the writ of *mort d'ancestor* cited above,[48] would also have had the effect of transferring cases to his court. A few years earlier (between 1208 and 1213) the earl's sometime chancellor Peter the clerk had been granted 'his own court free from all pleas and causes, except for pleas pertaining to my sword' - precisely the concession which featured here in the earl's great charter[49] - and there may well have been a sense that what Ranulf was prepared to grant to his favourites should be put in writing for the benefit of the baronial community at large. But the statement reads more like one of general principle than a negotiated response to a specific, acutely-felt grievance.

The next part of the clause, however, has a rather different character, addressing a particular procedure whereby lords could 'reclaim' those from their estates who had been arrested for a criminal offence by securing bail for them; it does so in a manner which suggests genuine concern about current practice. This type of reclaiming was otherwise known as 'replevying'. Imprisonment pending trial was an expensive option and not always secure, so the granting of bail with guarantees that the accused would duly appear to answer the charges was a well-established practice across the kingdom. The legal treatise of *c*.1188 known to historians as 'Glanvill' took for granted that it was unnecessary to put an arrested person in gaol if 'pledges' (otherwise translated as 'sureties') came

---

[47] *CEC*, nos. 267, 286, 375 (cf. 377-78, with the same concession to Dieulacres abbey after the Cheshire Magna Carta had been issued).
[48] *CEC*, no. 397.
[49] *CEC*, no. 282. Cf. the restriction to the earl's court of 'pleas of the sword' in the charter of liberties for Frodsham, *CEC*, no. 371, and also in no. 374 (although of questionable authenticity).

forward to guarantee an appearance in court. Roughly two decades earlier, legislation known as the Assize of Clarendon, targeted especially at notorious criminals, had provided that 'if the lord of the man who has been arrested, or his steward or his vassals shall claim him by pledge within the third day following his capture, let him be released on bail with his chattels until he himself shall stand his trial'. Both statements were made in the context of 'crown pleas', the most serious crimes, although 'Glanvill' made an exception of homicide and by the mid-thirteenth century this, alongside forest offences and certain unspecified 'other causes', were regarded as irreplevisable: no amount of 'pledges' were sufficient to secure bail. 'Glanvill' also explains that the 'pledges' were liable to a financial penalty if the alleged criminal failed to appear on the day appointed for trial.[50]

One feature of thirteenth-century Cheshire - also found in Wales, Scotland and parts of northern England and the marches but certainly not the kingdom as a whole - was the presence of 'serjeants of the peace', a rudimentary police force responsible for apprehending criminals and in some cases serving as prosecutors in court.[51] Clause 11 of Ranulf's great charter, to be considered below, portrays the earl's serjeants as riding around the county enforcing law and order while living at the expense of the landholding community at large. However, the Cheshire barons also had their own serjeants patrolling their own estates, and they too expected to be fed off the produce of the land; in the following century, the baron of Dunham, Sir Hamo de Mascy, had six of them, while his counterpart at Halton, Henry duke of Lancaster, had a master-serjeant and eight others. There was clearly potential in all this for confrontations over the arrest of thieves and

---

[50] *Glanvill*, ed. Hall, pp. 8 n. 1, 20, 171-72; *EHD*, II, no. 24 (cap. 3); Pollock and Maitland, *History of English Law*, II, pp. 185 n. 2, 584-86.
[51] R. Stewart-Brown, *The Serjeants of the Peace in Medieval England and Wales* (Manchester, 1936), esp. pp. 3-25 and cf. for Scotland A. Grant, 'Franchises north of the border: Baronies and regalities in medieval Scotland' in M. Prestwich, ed., *Liberties and Identities in the Medieval British Isles* (Woodbridge, 2008), pp. 155-98, at pp. 179-80.

other alleged criminals, disputes over whose serjeants ought to have made an arrest and whose courts the offenders ended up in as a result.[52]

There is inevitably a measure of speculation here but this could have been the context for the concession which the Cheshire barons secured in this second part of the opening clause. If the earl's serjeants were being over-zealous in arresting the barons' men and those who dwelt on their estates - sometimes for offences which the barons thought should have come before their own courts - there would have been acute resentment at having to pay to bail them out of the earl's jurisdiction. If so, the promise that these men could be bailed 'without ransom' would have gone some way towards appeasing the barons. But bail was not the end of the story. If any of a lord's men 'shall be taken for any offence' by one of the earl's serjeants, the case would remain with the county court - the earl's court - where the lord would have to present the alleged offender three times; he would then be acquitted unless a 'sacraber' came forward on one of those occasions to lay an accusation against him. 'Sacraber' (otherwise 'sacrabar') is a word probably of Scandinavian origin - it is only found in parts of the country within or close to the former Danelaw - denoting a private prosecutor, suing the defendant as (or on behalf of) the victim of the alleged offence.[53] His role served as a further safeguard against vexatious conduct by the earl's serjeants, since court proceedings could only begin on a private accusation, not one brought by a serjeant.

---

[52] Ormerod, *History of the County Palatine* (1882), I, pp. 526, 704; Stewart-Brown, *Serjeants of the Peace*, pp. 19-23.

[53] An older interpretation that the sacraber was a 'public prosecutor in a shire or [its subdivision, a] hundred' (D.M. Stenton, *English Justice between the Norman Conquest and the Great Charter*, London, 1965, pp. 55-56) has been rejected as a result of the arguments in J.M. Kaye, 'The Sacrabar', *EHR*, LXXXIII (1968), pp. 744-58; cf. Holt, *Magna Carta*, pp. 67-68. A sacraber appears as a figure distinct from the earl's officials in *CEC*, no. 209 (*c*.1190-1200).

Overall, this clause reads as if it was the product of careful negotiation, striking a balance between the concerns of the earl and those of his barons. The barons' entitlement in principle to jurisdiction over their tenants and those who dwelt on their estates is affirmed, but so is the earl's to deal with the most serious criminal offences. A specific grievance over the activities of the earl's serjeants is then tackled. If they have arrested any of the barons' men, jurisdiction will remain with the earl's county court, but the barons can bail them at no cost provided that they undertake to bring them back to court, and any case against them will rest on a private prosecution by (or on behalf of) the victim, not on the word of the arresting serjeant. If this interpretation is correct, there is some similarity with clause 38 of the Runnymede Magna Carta:

> Henceforth, no bailiff will put anyone on trial by his own unsupported allegation, without bringing credible witnesses to the charge.

The same anxiety about unsupported accusations by public officials would surface again - even more convincingly - in clause 4 of Ranulf's charter, to be discussed below.

Clause 2

The second clause related to the respective claims of the earl and his barons to 'avowers', strangers from elsewhere in the kingdom who had come to settle in Cheshire seeking the protection of a lord. Back in 1129-30, when Ranulf II earl of Chester had confirmed his tenant Hugh son of Odard in his holding, he had added specific protection for 'Uttlet and his children and his wife, and Algar and his children and his wife' who had evidently arrived on the estate, which was based at Dutton on the River Weaver. About four decades later, we find Ranulf II's son Earl Hugh entering into formal agreements with his barons over the admission of incomers, one with Warin de Vernon who gave the earl four marks (£2, 13s. 4d.) to settle four named men and their families, another with William de Venables in respect of a further two.[54] These charters suggest that the 'avowry' system, entitling Cheshire barons to settle and protect outsiders on their estates, was already well-established by Ranulf III's time, if not perhaps fully evolved; it is quite possible that the more systematic pursuit of criminals initiated by Henry II's Assize of Clarendon in 1166, a deliberate 'drive against crime' requiring the co-operation of sheriffs and the king's itinerant justices, had increased the number of fugitives from justice entering the county.[55] As it stands, clause 2 reads as a written guarantee of existing customary practice, with the earl taking the opportunity to assert his own claims to those who specifically sought his protection while confirming his barons' rights as well. It is only in the following clause that we have any indication of possible dispute between the earl and his barons in this area.

Medieval peasants, including those supposedly 'tied to their manor' as unfree villeins, were far from immobile. With the rapid increase in England's population in the two centuries prior to 1300, developments such as the growth of towns and the proliferation of new settlements depended on large numbers of individuals and families being able and willing to move away from their places of birth. Mobility continued during the population downturn of the fourteenth and fifteenth centuries, as economic prospects for the reduced number of peasants improved, so encouraging migration in search of the best possible terms.[56] Some outsiders who settled in Cheshire, certainly during the twelfth and thirteenth centuries, were

---

[54] *CEC*, nos. 15, 160, 162; G. Barraclough, 'Some Charters of the Earls of Chester' in P.M. Barnes and C.F. Slade, ed., *A Medieval Miscellany for Doris Mary Stenton* (Pipe Roll Society, new series, XXXVI, 1962 for 1960), pp. 25-43, at pp. 35-37.

[55] The Assize of Clarendon had provided for those of ill repute to abjure the realm, even though they had been cleared of their crimes; cap. 6 of the 'Inquest of Sheriffs' of 1170 had concerned 'the chattels of those who have fled on account of the Assize of Clarendon' (*EHD*, II, nos. 24, 48).

[56] See e.g. C. Dyer, *Making a Living in the Middle Ages* (London, 2003), pp. 184, 188-90, 304-10, 350-52.

welcomed because of the boost they offered to an under-populated countryside; according to Domesday Book in 1086, the county had fewer people per square mile than any shire in the Midlands or south of England, including Shropshire and Herefordshire further along the Welsh border.[57] But others, as the reference in this clause to 'transgressions' makes clear, arrived as fugitives from justice and this seems to have become the principal motivation as the Middle Ages wore on. What distinguished Cheshire from the rest of the kingdom was the custom - evidently in place by Ranulf II's time though its origins are obscure - whereby strangers could specifically be offered protection, against those who wished to bring them to justice and against any former lords who wished to reclaim them for their estates. In return, the settlers paid an annual sum for that protection to their new lords and - at least by the thirteenth century - their menfolk seem usually to have been liable for military service.[58]

The right to accommodate these settlers was of some financial importance. At Castle Shotwick in 1280, payments by 'avowers' were bringing in 5s. 6d. per annum to the lord, at 4d. per head; at Darnhall in 1291, the total sum was 2s. 0d. per annum. The grand annual income to the earl from this source around that time exceeded £30, peaking at £48 in 1308: a figure from which a total of well over 2,000 individual contributors has been extrapolated. However, despite the provision in Ranulf III's great charter that strangers should be 'trustworthy', Cheshire society as a whole inevitably suffered the consequences of harbouring escaped criminals who were being kept ready for war. Certain tracts of land were assigned as places where these people could settle temporarily, such as Overmarsh (otherwise King's Marsh) near Farndon, described in an early fourteenth-century inquisition as 'for the dwelling-place of foreigners ... seeking the

---

[57] H.C. Darby, *Domesday England* (Cambridge, 1977), pp. 90-91; P.J. Morgan, *War and Society in Medieval Cheshire, 1277-1403* (Chetham Society, 3rd Series, XXXIV, 1987), p. 80.
[58] R. Stewart-Brown, 'The Avowries of Cheshire', *EHR*, XXIX (1914), pp. 41-55.

protection of the Earl of Chester or coming to his aid in time of war'.[59] But they inevitably had a disruptive effect beyond these confines and there must have been widespread relief when the avowry system was finally abolished in 1542. By then, however, much smaller numbers were involved and it had degenerated into a device for avoiding repayment of debts.[60]

Clause 3

If clause 2 enabled the earl to define some of his own rights, clause 3 did so even more emphatically. It opens with a statement not of the Cheshire barons' entitlements but of their obligations to him as their lord, in circumstances where attacks on the county from Wales were a recurrent threat. There were only about 80 knights' fees in the whole of the county, a figure which helps to explain both the insistence here on the maximum turn-out and the attraction of settling 'avowers' as a supplementary force.[61] 'When need may require in war', barons and the knights who held fees (fiefs or tenancies) from them should perform the military service due for them in full, if necessary through providing a substitute; the reference to breastplates and haubergeons (otherwise hauberks, or tunics of chain mail) presumably meant that every knight and free tenant must provide his own, in readiness to defend his own property. But the clause then reverted to the subject of avowries, as if Ranulf had had to make concessions in return for the barons' commitment to their full military service.

---

[59] Morgan, *War and Society*, p. 80.
[60] Stewart-Brown, 'Avowries', pp. 48, 50-51, 54-55. The sheriff accounted for £16 arising from 'avowries' in 1349, a sum which (presumably because of the Black Death) had dropped by over half to £7, 6s. 8d. a year later: *Accounts of the Chamberlains and other Officers of the County of Chester, 1301-1360*, ed. R. Stewart-Brown (Record Society of Lancashire and Cheshire, LIX, 1910), pp. 133, 171.
[61] *Red Book of the Exchequer*, ed. H. Hall (Rolls Series, London, 1896), I, p. 184; *Chartulary of St Werburgh, Chester*, ed. Tait, I, p. 108.

The impression given by the final part of this clause is that Ranulf had been trying to deprive his barons of control over some of the villeins (unfree peasants) on their estates and had been seeking to secure military service from them. The barons' villeins were now to be acquitted ('quit') of any obligation to fight directly for the earl. In particular, his release to the barons of those villeins who 'came to my avowry through Ranulf de Davenham' implies an arrangement for the reception of strangers which had led to the barons feeling cheated of their expectations; perhaps Davenham, an occasional witness to the earl's charters over a decade before, had been acting as some sort of agent and had channelled the incomers away from the barons' estates and towards those of the earl.[62] This can be no more than speculation, but Ranulf had been actively campaigning against the Welsh between 1209 and 1212 - at one stage having to be rescued by his constable John de Lacy when trapped at Twt Hill, Rhuddlan - and his decision to move the monks of Poulton to the safer confines of Dieulacres near Leek in 1214 was prompted, at least in part, by their vulnerability to Welsh incursions.[63] In these circumstances, anxious for more soldiers, he might well have been trying to exploit the 'avowry' system to his own advantage, so as not to have to rely too heavily on a supply from his barons. If so, the barons clearly objected, but in the negotiations which followed the earl at least secured the guarantee of his full service entitlement with which the clause began.

Clause 4

This short clause introduces some unfamiliar terms and poses problems of interpretation, but in essence it is another example of the barons seeking to safeguard their jurisdiction over those who dwelt on

---

[62] *CEC*, nos. 223, 245, 256-57; in *Chartulary of St Werburgh, Chester*, I, p. 103, note 12, Tait suggests that he may have been 'keeper of the avowries' but does not elaborate.
[63] Soden, *Ranulf de Blondeville*, pp. 55-57; R. Swallow, 'Palimpsest of Border Power: The Archaeological Survey of Dodleston Castle, Cheshire', *Cheshire History*, LIV (2014-15), pp. 24-51, at pp. 28-29.

their estates. 'Thwertnic', which appears in some other medieval texts as 'thwert-ut-nay', was an English expression ultimately derived from Old Norse and meant a 'thorough no' (that is, 'I deny it all').[64] It was a phrase which an accused person could utter as a defence against a criminal charge and has been described as being similar to the plea that there is 'no case to answer'.[65] As for 'sirevestoth', the charter suggests that it was an annual payment by the Cheshire barons in return for the right of those from their estates to use this defence, although it may have covered other privileges as well. The clause is concerned to guarantee the right to the 'thwertnic' defence for any of the barons' men accused in the earl's court by the sheriff or other officer, although there is provision lest 'the suit pursues him', a phrase to which we shall return.

In early-thirteenth-century England as a whole, most criminal cases actually began, not with a charge laid by a 'public' official such as a sheriff but with a private accusation by (or on behalf of) the alleged victim: the 'sacraber' of clause 1 wherever this term had local currency. Most of these prosecutions, in turn, were not eventually pursued, or ended in a compromise settlement in or out of court. However, the formal procedure was for the accuser's 'appeal' to be answered either with an admission of guilt or by a point-by-point denial, after which the court could either decide on an obvious verdict or proceed - usually on a future occasion - to test the accuser's 'proofs'. Such tests might include the testimony of a 'suit' of witnesses, sworn declarations by 'oath-helpers' to affirm the truth of what one or other party had said, a sworn inquest by a jury of knowledgeable neighbours, a judicial duel ('trial by battle') or the submission of the accused to the ordeal of iron or water (although this

[64] *Middle English Dictionary, part T.6* (Ann Arbor, 1995), p. 675.
[65] R. Stewart-Brown, 'Thwert-ut-Nay and the Custom of "Thwertnic" in Cheshire', *EHR*, XL (1925), pp. 13-21; P. Hyams, 'Orality and Literacy in the Age of the Angevin Law Reforms' in R.E. Kaeuper, ed., *Law, Governance and Justice: New Views on Medieval Constitutionalism* (Leiden, 2013), pp. 27-72, at pp. 39-40.

was quickly dropped after condemnation at the Fourth Lateran Council in 1215).[66] In the light of how all this played out, judgment would eventually be passed.

'Thwertnic' cut through some of this by allowing the accused to make a blanket denial of the charge. At the most basic level, this could be an advantage to the defendant since (s)he was spared the necessity to answer point-by-point, which carried the risk of being judged guilty without more ado through failing to respond properly on some matter of detail. References to 'thwertnic' are so infrequent in accounts of medieval lawsuits that it cannot have been other than an occasional, localised, custom, again possibly associated with an origin in the Danelaw,[67] but what evidence we have shows that it did not, in itself, bring a case to an end. In Leicester in the 1270s, it was the obligatory form of denial in the town court, but only as a prelude to the testing of the proofs.[68] As for thirteenth-century Cheshire, it occurs in a variety of cases which add considerably to our understanding of the process, beyond what can be gleaned from the brief statement in Earl Ranulf's great charter.

In the records of the county court, we find, for example, that it was available as a defence against private prosecutions, not only those brought by one of the earl's officials as implied by the charter. Thus, in 1260, Cadogan de Hadley accused Richard de Bromhall of 'a premeditated assault ... with a bow and an axe' which had led to the

---

[66] Pollock and Maitland, *History of English Law*, II, pp. 598-99, 603-19, 642-43; Hudson, *Formation*, pp. 69-77, 170-79; Hudson, *Oxford History of the Laws*, pp. 303-32. *Glanvill*, ed. Hall, p. 173, envisaged water as the ordeal for unfree peasants and the hot iron as the ordeal for the free but *English Lawsuits*, II, nos. 471, 493, 520 show flexibility of practice. The former involved lowering the accused into a pit to see if (s)he floated or sank - floating meant guilty - while the latter depended on whether the wound caused by carrying the iron had healed within a specified time.

[67] Kaye, 'The Sacrabar', p. 745.

[68] *Records of the Borough of Leicester*, ed. M. Bateson (London, 1899), pp. 156-60.

death of Cadogan's nephew; de Bromhall had earlier responded by 'twertinhc' but now changed tack, claiming that as a clerk in holy orders he was subject to a church court instead. A defendant might pay for permission to use the device, rather than rely on the customary render of 'sirevestoth'. This happened at Macclesfield in 1286, when the earl's justiciar Reginald de Grey was hearing forest cases: 'William de Chisseworth, taken on suspicion, denied and gave [6s. 8d.] ... for leave to answer by the denial called "Twertnik" according to the custom of the country'. There might be occasions when the defence was not allowed, as in 1260 when Ralph de Mouldsworth and his wife Margaret, accused of murder, were told by the justiciar that their 'twertnic' responses did not meet the case; in the same year, Judde Clubbe, an alleged murderer and arsonist who also answered by 'twertnik', was told the same thing.[69] Most significantly from the perspective of Earl Ranulf's charter, 'thwertnic' seems usually to have been associated with an entitlement for the Cheshire barons to claim defendants for their own 'liberties', although this was rarely the end of the matter. The Chisseworth case, cited above, was possibly the exception, involving a man who dwelt on the earl's estate, not that of one of the barons: hence the need for a special payment equivalent to perhaps eight or nine weeks' wages for an agricultural labourer.[70]

The clearest example of procedure is to be found among Reginald de Grey's Macclesfield forest cases in 1286, when, according to the record, 'Richard Baune, charged with being a receiver of poachers, answered by "twertnik" according to the common liberty of the country'; at this, Adam de Burton, 'the steward's bailiff' (acting for the baron of Mold Roger de Montalt, whose family were the earl's hereditary stewards) successfully claimed him 'for the liberty of his lord'. Richard was subsequently

---

[69] *Calendar of Court Rolls of Chester*, ed. Stewart-Brown, pp. 8 (no. 54), 10, 27, 226, and for Judde Clubbe see above on clause 1.

[70] G. Clark, 'The long march of history: farm wages, population, and economic growth, England 1209-1869', *Economic History Review*, LX (2007), pp. 97-135, at p. 99.

brought four times before the county court and eventually acquitted.[71] A broadly-similar sequence of events was played out time and again. A generation earlier, in the county court at Chester in 1259, William de Bostock, who held from the 'baron of Shipbrook', successfully used the 'thertnig' defence against an accusation laid by Sir Thomas de Orreby, who had recently been appointed the earl's warden of forests. Early in the following year, two men accused of stealing oxen from Thomas le Botiler of Minshull 'defended by "thuertnik" at the liberty of the constable', the post held hereditarily by the Lacy family, barons of Halton; they were acquitted. Also in 1260, Henry Battok, evidently in possession of a dead robber's chattels, was acquitted of any offence after thrice defending himself 'by "twertnic" at the liberty of the constable'. Another of the defendants in the Macclesfield forest pleas of 1286, Randle lord of Alsager, was indicted for being found in a wood with dogs but 'answered by "Twertnik" according to the custom of the country, denying everything alleged'; at this, 'Richard Starky, the constable's bailiff, claimed him for his lord's liberty according to the manner of the country' and he subsequently appeared at four county courts before being acquitted.[72] Richard de Bromhall, Judde Clubbe, Ralph de Mouldsworth and his wife Margaret, all of whom we have met previously attempting to use the 'thwertnic' defence, did so as within the liberty of the steward.

Yet another to defend himself 'by "Twertnic" at the liberty of the steward' was Henry the smith of Davenport, again in 1260, and this time we are given a few more glimpses of the procedure. The appeal in his case is stated to have been made by the coroners - officers of the earl as envisaged in Ranulf's charter - since 'it was rumoured' that Henry the smith was responsible for the death of Alecok the shepherd of Davenport, whose body had been found in the fields. Henry came to the court three times to use the 'thwertnic'

---

[71] *Calendar of Court Rolls of Chester*, ed. Stewart-Brown, p. 227, and cf. similar cases on the same page.
[72] *Calendar of Court Rolls of Chester*, ed. Stewart-Brown, pp. 2, 11, 24, 227; Stewart-Brown, 'Thwert-ut-Nay', p. 18.

defence and was duly acquitted, but an inquest jury from the township was still called upon to declare that 'it was a mischance'. In the same year, Eynon son of Sanne 'stole a hive of bees from Roger Arnold ... at the steward's liberty he defended himself by "Twertnic" the first time'. On his second appearance in court, however, he seems to have opted for the verdict of an inquest jury, and was acquitted as a result.[73]

Some important conclusions stem from all this. One is that 'thwertnic' could be used as a defence against both lesser and serious crimes, but not against every accusation. On the one hand, we find it applied with success in cases of receiving poachers and trespassing with dogs in the earl's forest,[74] and on the other in cases relating to certain thefts and homicides specifically stated to be 'pleas of the crown' (successor following Henry III's annexation of the earldom to the previous 'pleas of the sword').[75] It was not, however, allowed to alleged murderers like Judde Clubbe[76] and it may well be that, as we saw with 'replevying' in clause 1, a line was drawn at what were deemed the most serious offences of all.

Another major lesson concerns the role of 'thwertnic' in releasing the defendants to the 'liberties' of their baronial lords. Later government inquests into the holdings of the steward, the constable and also the baron of Dunham include this mode of defence as one of the privileges they enjoyed and it was clearly valued highly.[77] We are back to the first clause, with the barons anxious to free their tenants and those who dwelt on their estates from the clutches of the earl's court, as far as they could; indeed, in the case of Judde Clubbe in 1260, his lord attempted to reclaim him via the 'replevying' process of

---

[73] *Calendar of Court Rolls of Chester*, ed. Stewart-Brown, p. 33, 28; cf, pp. 8 (no. 49), 28 (no. 211) for other 'thwertnic' defences which may have been followed by a further process before acquittal.
[74] *Calendar of Court Rolls of Chester*, ed. Stewart-Brown, p. 227.
[75] *Calendar of Court Rolls of Chester*, ed. Stewart-Brown, pp. 11, 27, 28, 33.
[76] *Calendar of Court Rolls of Chester*, ed. Stewart-Brown, pp. 8 (no. 54), 10.
[77] Stewart-Brown, 'Thwert-ut-Nay', p. 21.

clause 1 after 'thwertnic' had been disallowed, though with equal lack of success.[78] There were differences between the two devices, however. 'Replevying' was an action taken by the lord, usually (it seems, and despite the Clubbe case) before the accused had come to trial. 'Thwertnic', on the other hand, was a defence used by the accused once a charge had been brought, though sometimes with the connivance of the lord. Even so, the effect could be much the same. Under either process, judgment remained with the earl's county court before which the accused was required to make repeated appearances, but the onus was thrown back on the prosecution. Clause 1, as we have seen, makes it clear that a private appeal by a 'sacraber' could still be laid. As for clause 4, an authoritative interpretation of the phrase 'unless the suit pursues him' is that this meant the same thing, the 'suit' being one made against a defendant by a private accuser.[79] However, if this was the case, it is hard to understand why the word 'suit' (Latin: *secta*) was used in clause 4 instead of the 'sacraber' of clause 1. An alternative explanation is that the reference is to a 'suit of witnesses'; once 'thwertnic' had been pleaded a case could only proceed if there were credible witnesses to support the charge, as in clause 38 of the Runnymede Magna Carta, quoted above at the end of the discussion of clause 1.[80] While this must remain uncertain, there can be no doubt that 'thwertnic' did leave open the possibility of some further process to test the guilt of the accused, as in the cases of Henry the smith and Eynon son of Sanne above, where inquest juries finally settled the matter.

---

[78] *Calendar of Court Rolls of Chester*, ed. Stewart-Brown, p. 10, where Judde Clubbe and his men's lord (the earl's hereditary steward, represented by his bailiff) tried to 'replevy' them after the 'thwertnic' defence had been disallowed, only for the justiciar to disallow this as well. For 'replevying' even after an accusation had formally been made in court, see Pollock and Maitland, *History of English Law*, II, p. 584.

[79] Kaye, 'The Sacrabar', p. 754.

[80] This also appears to be the view expressed by Tait in *Chartulary of St Werburgh, Chester*, I, pp. 101, 108.

A final issue is whether release to the 'liberty' of the lord left the defendant liable to fresh prosecution for the same offence in the relevant baronial court. Previous interpretations of the clause, while differing in some respects, have concluded that cases successfully defended by 'thwertnic' in the earl's county court might indeed subsequently be pursued in a baronial court[81] but how far this applied in practice is questionable. 'Pleas of the sword', whether or not they generated a 'thwertnic' defence, were supposed to be concluded in the earl's court in any case, as clause 1 of Ranulf's charter makes clear; it is hard to see how these could have been re-opened in one of the barons' courts. Insofar as lesser offences, which might have come to a baronial court in the first place, now found themselves back in the lord's jurisdiction, there was the question of whether a prosecution which had already failed in a superior court was worth re-opening, unless the baron was particularly keen to be rid of some troublesome individual. By the fourteenth century, as we shall see in a moment, 'thwertnic' was certainly being seen as a means for criminals to escape justice, and it is unlikely that this reputation would have arisen if there had been consistent and rigorous follow-up, on the part of the barons, of cases remitted to their courts in this way.

So - with one eye on processes as described in the later court rolls - we may paraphrase clause 4 as follows:

> If the sheriff or any officer of the earl's court shall accuse one of the barons' men of a criminal offence, he may defend himself by the statement 'I deny it all', which in return for an annual levy automatically removes him to his lord's control. (Much as in clause 1) a man who has pleaded 'I deny it all' will still have to be presented to a specified number of meetings of the earl's county court but will be acquitted unless there is support for the charge.

---

[81] Stewart-Brown, 'Thwert-ut-Nay', p. 20; Kaye, 'The Sacrabar', p. 754.

It must be added at once that this interpretation remains speculative. The inconclusive nature of the evidence means that a measure of disagreement is all but inevitable. But whatever the precise meaning of the procedures described in this clause, we should dismiss any notion that Earl Ranulf's great charter was responsible for introducing 'thwertnic' to Cheshire. As described in the accounts of the Macclesfield forest cases, it was part of the 'custom' or 'common liberty of the country' (i.e. the county), of unknown origin, and we have seen that its application in the thirteenth-century courts went well beyond the provisions made in clause 4; it embraced cases brought by accusers other than the earl's officers and it evidently extended to those who were not the barons' men, provided that they were willing to pay. Clause 4 focused on a particular application of 'thwertnic' - where comital officials were accusing baronial dependants - and its provisions may not have been new, especially since 'sirevestoth', which was apparently paid in return for the arrangement, occurs some years earlier.[82] As with the first part of clause 1, the concession may largely be a response to a bid by the barons to have their own particular stake in the 'thwertnic' process enshrined in writing; in seeking this, they may well have been prompted - as in clause 1 - by irritation at the activities of overbearing officers of the earl, who were thought to be arresting too many 'barons' men', so depleting the manpower on their estates. 'Thwertnic' sat alongside the 'replevying' of clause 1 as a means to claim their men back from the earl's court. The downside, from the point of view of the maintenance of law and order, was that it was arguably too easy a defence for the notorious criminal against whom no-one wished to come forward to corroborate a charge. This drawback would have been compounded if, in practice, there was rarely any follow-up elsewhere, once the earl's county court had dismissed the case.

---

[82] *CEC*, no. 245 (dated 1193-1203); cf. no. 434 (*c*.1230) for a later grant of exemption from what is there expressed as 'shirrevestude'.

Yet if we know nothing of how or when 'thwertnic' originated in Cheshire, we do know about its end. As late as autumn 1350 - when the Black Death was in full swing - the sheriff was still collecting 'sirevestoth' as a levy from the five hundreds of Cheshire, totalling £5 0s. 4½d. per annum.[83] By then, however, there was clearly a perception - doubtless linked to the 'avowry' system with its encouragement to criminals to take refuge in the county - that 'thwertnic' was frustrating prosecutions and contributing to prevailing lawlessness. In a charter of 10 September 1353, Edward the Black Prince, in his capacity as earl of Chester, formally abolished it, abrogating clause 4 of the charter at the same time. It was a custom 'contrary to the common law and is the origin of trouble and destructive to peace' so 'this defence shall not be allowed in future and the said charter in that point shall be of no effect'.[84]

Clause 5

This is a relatively straightforward clause, with the barons securing the abolition of some payments and a cap on others. The exaction of sheaves is a small pointer reinforcing the well-established argument that cereal-growing was an important part of the rural economy of medieval Cheshire, at least before the middle of the fourteenth century.[85] Indeed, by 1220 at the latest, Earl Ranulf III seems to have

---

[83] *Accounts of the County of Chester*, ed. Stewart-Brown, pp. 133, 171.

[84] Stewart-Brown, 'Thwert-ut-Nay', p. 20, with the date corrected in *Calendar of Court Rolls of Chester*, ed. Stewart-Brown, p. xxxi, n. 2; P.H.W. Booth, *The Financial Administration of the Lordship and County of Chester, 1272-1377* (Chetham Society, 3rd series, XXVIII, 1981), p. 122.

[85] See e.g. A.D.M. Phillips and C.D. Phillips, *A New Historical Atlas of Cheshire* (Chester, 2002), p. 34. There is a resemblance, noted in *Chartulary of St Werburgh, Chester*, ed. Tait, I, p. 108, between this concession and clause 28 of the Runnymede Magna Carta, which states that any corn taken must be paid for in cash (cf. the commentary on clause 11, below); however this was addressing the specific issue of purveyance, i.e. the requisitioning of supplies for the royal household (McKechnie, *Magna Carta*, pp. 329-33).

become the first earl of Chester to adopt wheatsheaves as a device on his shield.[86] The concession anticipates a similar one in Henry III's Charter of the Forest of 1217,[87] discussed in connection with the next clause, that 'no forester or beadle shall henceforth ... levy sheaves of corn'. Clearly, the requirement to hand over a share of a hard-won resource to the earl's officers was a source of resentment and this was one Cheshire 'custom' the barons were only too glad to be rid of.

The second part of this clause dealt with amercements (financial penalties) imposed on the personnel of the hundred and county courts - we may safely assume as punishment for non-attendance.[88] A distinction was drawn between 'judges' (sometimes called doomsmen) and 'suitors', both roles attached to specific landholdings. In the case of 'judges', these properties were mostly military tenancies held directly from the earl, although the obligation could be passed to a sub-tenant under the terms of a grant of land. The finding of 'suitors', however, was incumbent upon a wide range of lesser holdings, some held by those we would consider free peasants. The hierarchy of courts depended on these people's participation. 'Suitors' bore witness to what had happened in their localities while 'judges' made crucial decisions on the basis of the evidence before them - sometimes on how a case should proceed, sometimes on the guilt or innocence of the accused, sometimes on rightful tenure of land in dispute - albeit under the presidency of the justiciar of Chester if cases were heard in the earl's county court.[89]

---

[86] T.A. Heslop, 'The Seals of the Twelfth-Century Earls of Chester' in Thacker, ed., *Earldom of Chester and its Charters*, pp. 179-97, at pp. 194-95.
[87] *EHD*, III, ed. H. Rothwell (2nd edn,, London, 1995), no. 24 (cap. 7).
[88] For what follows, here and in the next paragraph, see esp. *Calendar of Court Rolls of Chester*, ed. Stewart-Brown, pp. xvi-xxvii, xxxii-xxxviii.
[89] It is because of their role in 'judging' rather than in presiding over the court that the term 'judger' is sometimes preferred to 'judge' as a translation of the Latin *iudex*, e.g. in *Calendar of Court Rolls of Chester*, ed. Stewart-Brown, p. xxxii and in *CEC*, pp. 322, 346-47, 398.

Artist's impression of Ranulf III's seal as earl of Chester and Lincoln around 1217-20, as reproduced in G. Ormerod, History of the County Palatine and City of Chester (1817), I, p. 41.

In the early thirteenth century, this county court met every six weeks, invariably at Chester castle, and as we have seen embraced within its range matters which elsewhere in England would have come before the king's itinerant justices; hundred courts assembled in their various local meeting-places at least once a month. So the obligation of attendance was a heavy one and clearly irksome to many of those involved. Release from it was a cherished privilege. For example, among the grants made to the hereditary forester of Leek and Macclesfield, Richard Davenport, sometime around 1210, were freedom from suit at the county court at Chester and hundred court of Northwich and freedom from having to find judges for these courts; reluctance to travel from the east of the county to meetings in Chester is evidently no new phenomenon! At a broadly similar date, the much-favoured Peter the clerk was released from having to do suit to the county and hundred courts, an obligation specifically attached to his holding of Thornton-le-Moors; if he granted the vill to someone else, the quittance would pass to the recipient.[90] In reality, it was common for the greater landholders to find substitutes to fulfil the duties of judge on their behalf, whether by special arrangement or through granting them holdings with the specific obligation attached: a practice which allowed the growth of what may be envisaged as a professional (and hereditary) group of committed attenders, knowledgeable about custom and precedent. Clause 10 of Henry III's so-called Statute of Merton in 1236 would give every free man the right to be represented at the shire court by a suitor on his behalf, but this seems to have been an extension of a privilege long enjoyed by the baronage of Cheshire, as well as by the barons of England as a whole.[91]

The concern in this clause about disproportionate amercements echoes to some extent clauses 20 and 21 of King John's Magna Carta:

. A free man will not be amerced for a trivial offence, except in accordance with the degree of the offence ...

---

[90] *CEC*, nos. 348 (dated 1207-13), 285 (1208-17); see also no. 321 (1200-03), freeing William Neville and his wife of any obligation attached to Longdendale to find a judge for the earl's court at Macclesfield (discussed under clause 7, below).

[91] Pollock and Maitland, *History of English Law*, I, p. 547; see below on clause 7.

Earls and barons will not be amerced except by their peers and only in accordance with the degree of the offence.

But whereas at Runnymede the issue had been amercements in general, the Cheshire charter focused on penalties specifically relating to obligations at court, restricting them to a sum well below the ten shillings which, according to Domesday Book, was liable to be imposed on a judge absent without excuse from the borough court of Chester.[92] As usual, we do not know if Earl Ranulf had in fact been collecting more than the sums laid down, but the fact that the judges (or strictly speaking those on whom the obligation to find a judge went with their landholdings) were to be amerced at double the figure imposed on the suitors is testimony to their greater importance. As an example of the custom in practice, we may cite the eyre roll for Macclesfield of October 1288, when 'the abbot of Dieulacres was called upon to show why he need not attend on the first day of the eyre'. 'He had no reply and must appear in future' but in the event he was pardoned the amercement because he was new to his office. Two years later, the townships of Alderley and Hattersley were each amerced 6s. 8d. 'for not coming with four men and the reeve at the summons of the eyre' to do their duty as suitors.[93] By the mid-fourteenth century, the sheriff was collecting over £11 per annum from judges and suitors absenting themselves from the county and hundred courts. However, the fact that for two of the hundreds, Wirral and Nantwich, the sums involved were identical from one year to the next, and for the remainder were very similar, strongly suggests that the system had by then evolved to a point where payments were

---

[92] *Domesday Book: Cheshire*, ed. P. Morgan (Chichester, 1978), 262 c, d.
[93] *Calendar of Court Rolls of Chester*, ed. Stewart-Brown, pp. 237, 240. The 'eyre', literally derived from the Latin word for 'journey', refers to the court held by the itinerant justice(s).

normally pre-arranged fines for permission to be released, rather than actual punishments.[94]

Clause 6

The administration of the county's forests was the next subject to be tackled.[95] The word 'forest' is ultimately derived from the Latin *foris*, 'outside'; it was a tract of land outside normal jurisdiction, being set aside as a hunting reserve with its own laws to protect the game (predominantly deer) and its own arrangements for law enforcement. Although Old English precedents have been found for William the Conqueror's designation of certain areas as 'forest', both their extent and the rigour of the laws applied within them increased markedly following the arrival of the Normans. By Henry II's reign it is reckoned that one third of the landed area of England was treated as 'forest', much of it actually in the tenure of barons and other freeholders rather than part of the king's own estate. The so-called Assize of the Forest (otherwise the Assize of Woodstock, a composite text of 1184 and later) provides a useful summary of regulations by the turn of the century, with stringent provisions to preserve woodland cover, prevent poaching and restrict grazing, all enforced by special forest justices.[96] Richard I and John actually reduced the extent of royal forest - charging local communities heavily for the concession - but anger at the intrusive interference with the management of estates persisted, allied to resentment about damage done by hunting parties and the imposition of a separate judicial regime. All this was of immediate - sometimes literally vital - concern to the peasants who made a living from the land but it affected also the lords and barons whose income from rents and produce was diminished.

---

[94] *Accounts of the County of Chester*, ed. Stewart-Brown, pp. 133, 171-72; cf. the fines for release from jury service also recorded here on pp. 134, 172.
[95] On what follows in this paragraph, see e.g. G.J. White, *The Medieval Landscape, 1000-1540* (London, 2012), pp. 44-45 and sources there cited.
[96] *EHD*, II, no. 28.

King John's Magna Carta devoted three clauses (nos. 44, 47 and 48) to the royal forests:

> Henceforth men who live outside the forest will not come before our justices of the forest upon a general summons, unless they are impleaded or are sureties for any person or persons who are attached for forest offences.

> All forests which have been afforested in our time will be disafforested at once …

> All evil customs of forests and warrens, foresters and warreners, sheriffs and their servants … are to be investigated at once … and within forty days of the inquiry such bad customs are to be abolished …

It is a measure of the strength of baronial feeling on this subject that in the reissues of Magna Carta in 1217 and 1225 (discussed below) they were superseded by separate Charters devoted exclusively to forest administration.

Although forests were usually fairly well-wooded, they could include a good deal of open countryside as well: moorland, heathland, even fenland, as well as settlements with their associated arable fields and pastures. Of the four forests in Cheshire by Ranulf III's time, covering about a third of the landed area of the county, Wirral had very little woodland recorded in Domesday Book, Delamere and Mondrem (on the mid-Cheshire ridge flanked by the Rivers Gowy and Weaver) rather more, while Macclesfield embraced Pennine moorland with wooded slopes below. All were, of course, areas of reserved hunting for the earl not the king, but the restrictions within them were broadly similar to those which applied in the rest of the country, so it is no surprise that the barons sought concessions arising from their experience in Cheshire. Interestingly, they did not press for any disafforestation of existing forests, or imply that officials had been abusing their positions, as at Runnymede, but focused on specific reforms which would yield them some benefit.

The first part of the clause granted the barons freedom to assart (that is, bring new land under cultivation, usually by clearing woodland or scrub) 'within the bounds of their husbandry' in the forest, which presumably meant as an extension to the cultivated land attached to one of the settlements on their estates. Provided the holding was their own, and the area to be cleared was immediately adjacent to already-cultivated land, they could cut down trees or otherwise interfere with the habitat of the beasts of the chase. The pipe rolls from Henry II's time onwards are full of payments made to the king for assarting, which demonstrates that it was certainly permitted in the rest of England at a price. The *Dialogue of the Exchequer*, an explanation of the central financial administration completed in 1179, describes the facility 'to cut down at pleasure [one's] own woods, in which the king's forest consists' in return for 'a perpetual rent of one shilling for each acre sown with wheat, and sixpence for each sown with oats' within the land brought into cultivation as a result; it also asserts the right of the 'barons of the exchequer' who presided over business to be quit of such levies on assarts made before 1135 and mentions the possibility of other exemptions by special permission of the king.[97] Two years after Magna Carta had been granted, the Charter of the Forest issued on behalf of the boy-king Henry III declared that all assarts made between 1154 and 1217 would be quit of future payments to the exchequer, though any new ones thereafter would still be chargeable.[98]

On the face of it, the Cheshire charter might suggest that assarting could now proceed in the earl's forests without any payment, provided that it involved an immediate extension of the cultivated area and did not reach beyond one's own estate. This was not in fact the

---

[97] Richard fitz Nigel, *Dialogus de Scaccario*, ed. C. Johnson, F.E.L. Carter and D.E. Greenway (Oxford, 1983), pp. 56-61.
[98] *EHD*, III, no. 24 (cap. 4).

case, since late-thirteenth and fourteenth-century evidence points to customary sums of 6s. 8d. and 5s. 0d. per acre as one-off payments at the first ploughing of the newly-assarted land; the difference related to its previous condition.[99] Even so, this was more generous than the fixed annual rent which applied in the rest of the country and the clause was similarly magnanimous in the matter of 'husbote' and 'haybote', the customary right to take wood for the repair of houses and fences (or hedges) respectively. According to the *Dialogue of the Exchequer* this required official supervision if exercised within the king's forests,[100] but the earl's charter makes clear that in his Cheshire forests it could go ahead without such oversight. The next concession - entitlement to give away or sell dead wood which had been collected - also represented a departure from the Assize of the Forest, where one could only collect for one's own needs, any right to 'give or sell' being expressly prohibited.[101] Seven decades later, when the justiciar was holding forest pleas at Macclesfield in January 1285, nine townships - among them Bollington, Gawsworth and Poynton - cited the charter 'granted by Ranulf earl of Chester and confirmed by the king' in defence of their practice of cutting down oaks without the foresters' supervision, obviously arguing that they were covered by

---

[99] *Accounts of the County of Chester*, ed. Stewart-Brown, pp. 131, 169 (Delamere and Mondrem); *VCH: Cheshire*, II, p. 169, esp. n. 25 for a Wirral claim that 5s. 0d. and 6s. 8d. related to previous acres of heath and woodland respectively. Cf. *Calendar of Court Rolls of Chester*, ed. Stewart-Brown, p. 212, where the Macclesfield eyre roll for 1285 records that Richard Kyde for assarting one acre of his lord's land and Hugh de Bosedon for assarting half an acre of his own land were both charged one-off sums of 5s. 0d. The statement in *VCH: Cheshire*, II, p. 169, that those who had assarted in Macclesfield forest paid an annual rent instead is based on *Calendar of Court Rolls of Chester*, ed. Stewart-Brown, pp. 223-25, to which pp. 212-13 could be added; however, the cases where annual rents are charged appear to relate to clearings made on the king's (otherwise the earl's) demesne, not those on one's own land or that of one's immediate lord.
[100] *Dialogus de Scaccario,* ed. Johnson *et al.*, p. 57.
[101] 'Assize of the Forest', cap. 3 in *EHD*, II, no. 28.

the provisions of this clause. 'The charter was inspected by the justiciar and the claim allowed.'[102]

All these concessions are relatively straightforward, but two other features of this clause pose significant problems of interpretation. One relates to the treatment of formerly-cultivated land, with the express prohibition of 'harbourage', the possible meanings of which are discussed in the next paragraph. The other is the last sentence, releasing the barons' men from impleading unless caught red-handed.

In different contexts, 'harbourage' (Latin: *herbergatio*) can refer to the procurement of accommodation, the lodging itself or an associated payment due. In a footnote to this clause for his 1920 edition of Earl Ranulf's charter, Tait was sympathetic to the view that the term meant a customary due, describing it as 'apparently a payment for cutting wood for building or repairing houses'. This would mean that permission was being granted for previously-cultivated land to be cultivated again, provided that it had not already reverted to woodland, free of any payment for cutting and taking building material. (If there was no wood in any case, there would be nothing to make the payment for.) The notion of 'exemption from payment' is an attractive one, though probably not payment for the activity specified by Tait, which was surely covered by the liberality already shown towards 'husbote'. An alternative explanation is exemption from having to make any customary payment for the right to build 'lodgings' on this previously-cultivated land.

However, there are difficulties with this interpretation. On the one hand, fourteenth-century account rolls mention pannage rent and 'frithmote' as customary payments due to the earl of Chester from his

---

[102] *Calendar of Court Rolls of Chester*, ed. Stewart-Brown, p. 213.

59

forests[103] but make no reference to 'herbergatio'; as a payment, it may by then have ceased to be levied, or it had come to bypass the foresters and chamberlains answerable for these accounts, but the most likely explanation is that it was not a payment at all. On the other hand, given the close control exercised by the earl - through his officers - over building in the forest, he could hardly be expected to waive a payment for permission to build. The Macclesfield eyre roll of 1286 makes it clear that houses erected in the forest without authorisation were liable to be pulled down, as was the case with royal forests elsewhere in the kingdom. To cite only one example:

> John the cook holds an acre of land ploughed up at Collegh' in Gawsworth in the soil of ... Thomas [de Orreby], and houses have been built thereon to the hurt of the forest. (Fine 5s.) The houses are to be thrown down, but the land may be held.[104]

Cases such as this make the more probable meaning of 'harbourage' in the context of this clause - a context in which it is specifically being denied - 'the right to build dwellings on the land'. This would render the concession to the effect that land left as waste but previously cultivated, not subject to any restrictions on assarting because it had not yet regained its tree cover, could be cultivated once again. However, the earl's customary control over new building would continue to apply and there would be no entitlement to build on the cultivated land.

The last part of the clause returned to the familiar theme of the respective jurisdictions of the earl and the barons over those who lived

---

[103] *Accounts of the Chamberlains*, ed. Stewart-Brown, pp. 2, 3, 16, 17, 32, 34, 35, etc.; both 'frithmote' and payments for pannage related to permission for livestock to feed in the forest.
[104] *Calendar of Court Rolls of Chester*, ed. Stewart-Brown, p. 225, cf. pp. 212, 224; cf. also *Select Pleas of the Forest*, ed. G.J. Turner (Selden Society, London, 1901), p. 18.

on baronial estates. For all the promises to the barons about clearing, cutting and collecting wood in the earl's forests, it would be their men who would be doing the hard work and they were duly acquitted of any possible forest offence which might arise as a result. There was not of course to be a free-for-all: a range of activities not covered by Ranulf's charter, notably poaching (and abetting poaching) but also illicit encroachments and failures to prevent the escape of animals, still featured among the offences dealt with at Macclesfield in the 1280s.[105] Of particular concern to the earl was that his foresters - his forest serjeants - should retain their rights over thieves caught in the act or found in possession of a bloody carcass. A poacher, for example, apprehended by the earl's foresters either killing game or with a dead beast over his shoulders, was liable to summary justice (quite possibly, execution), after the briefest of processes in the earl's court if not on the spot. These 'red-handed' thieves were precisely the people covered by the barons' customary rights of jurisdiction over their men discussed under clause 1, above, but by making an exception to the indemnity granted towards certain other activities, clause 6 appears to be saying that these baronial rights did not always apply if their men were arrested within the earl's forests; thieves caught in the forests red-handed were subject to the jurisdiction of the earl.[106] Here as elsewhere, Earl Ranulf was taking the opportunity to clarify his own entitlements as well as those of his barons.

There are no close parallels with any of these 'forest' concessions in the Runnymede Magna Carta, nor - with the partial

---

[105] *Calendar of Court Rolls of Chester*, ed. Stewart-Brown, pp. 212-14, 218, 224-28, 230-33.
[106] Pollock and Maitland, *History of English Law*, II, pp. 495 n. 4, 579. In *CEC*, no. 461, Ranulf's successor as earl in the 1230s, John le Scot, acquitted the monks of Stanlaw of certain aspects of forest justice in regard to Willington (in Delamere forest) but reserved his rights if they or their men were found with game or engaged in manifest transgression. Cf., however, the commentary on clause 4, above, where it is clear that the 'thwertnic' defence could be used in some forest cases.

exception of assarting - in the 1217 Charter of the Forest either. It seems clear, therefore, that the Cheshire barons were securing greater freedoms than their counterparts elsewhere, although as usual we cannot be sure how far these were 'new' promises, rather than written confirmations of established practice in the county. The fact that (in clause 12 to which we shall turn later on) the barons sought further liberties in the earl's forests, which Ranulf refused to grant, suggests that at least some of the concessions were newly-introduced, as part of the give and take of negotiation.

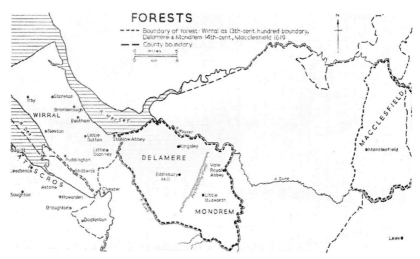

Cheshire's medieval forests. (Map reproduced from A History of the County of Chester, Vol. 2, p. 168, Oxford University Press, 1979, by permission of the Victoria County History.)

The barons would have been emboldened to submit their demands by the earl's track record of using his forests as a source of patronage. Around 1190-1200, for example, he had freed the monks of Stanlaw and their men from the attentions of the earl's foresters, following this some years later by 'disafforesting' their grange at Stanney; this meant, in effect, that farming could be conducted there without any reference to the laws protecting Wirral forest.[107] In the years immediately before issuing his great Cheshire charter, he had similarly 'disafforested' Barrow, a vill in Delamere forest held by his household officer Thomas Despenser.[108] Both Stanney and Barrow were on the very edges of their respective forests, so the boundaries were, in effect, being redrawn to exclude them. Among several examples of lesser concessions was one incorporated into the lengthy series granted in 1208-17 to the favourite Peter the clerk, whose vill of Thornton-le-Moors, in Wirral, was cleared of any liability to pay for pannage, the customary right to pasture pigs in the forest.[109] As we argued in connection with clause 1, it may well have been Earl Ranulf's readiness to surrender his entitlements in this or that respect, as a mark of special privilege, which created a climate in which the barons demanded equitable treatment for their group as a whole.

Clause 7

As noted in the discussion of clause 5, above, the right of barons to send a representative to the county court on their behalf had long been acknowledged across the country. It first appears in the so-called *Laws of Henry I*, an early twelfth-century legal treatise considered not to be an authoritative statement but an account of what the anonymous commentator thought significant about contemporary practice. This specifically names a baron's steward as entitled to speak for him in the county court.[110] Earl Ranulf's statement in his charter mentions the hundred court as well as that of the county and is adamant that one steward would be sufficient whatever the size of a holding, but it is hard to see this particular clause as anything more than a reaffirmation of existing practice. Between 1200 and 1203, Ranulf confirmed

---

[107] *CEC*, nos. 209, 211, cf. no. 215.
[108] *CEC*, no. 357 and on the Despensers, Crouch, 'Administration', pp. 78-79.
[109] *CEC*, no. 285; cf. e.g. nos. 342, 371, 384, 408.
[110] *Leges Henrici Primi*, ed. L.J. Downer (Oxford, 1972), pp. 100-101; *EHD*, II, no. 57 (cap. VII, 7, 7a). Cf. *Dialogus de Scaccario,* ed. Johnson *et al.*, pp. 116-17 for the steward's role in representing his baronial lord.

Longdendale to William Neville and his wife, adding that when William was summoned to the earl's court at Macclesfield his steward could appear in his place. However, this charter has several unusual features and the apparent wish to mention the steward's role as a specific concession does not mean that the practice was not already well-established among the Cheshire baronage as a whole.[111]

Clause 8

Several issues of acute concern to the barons of England surfaced in this clause. Indeed, it addressed matters covered in four different clauses of King John's Magna Carta (nos. 2, 6, 7 and 8) and touched on those in another (26):

> If any of our earls or barons or others holding of us in chief by knight service should die, and at his death his heir is of full age and owes relief, he will have his inheritance by the ancient relief, namely the heir or heirs of an earl £100 from a whole earl's barony, the heir or heirs of a baron £100 from a whole barony, and the heir or heirs of a knight at most 100 shillings from a whole knight's fee, and anyone who owes less will give less according to the ancient custom of fees.
>
> Heirs will be married without disparagement, save that before a marriage is contracted it be made known to the heir's close kin.
>
> After her husband's death, a widow will have her marriage portion and her inheritance at once and without any difficulty, nor will she pay anything for her dower, for her marriage portion, or for her inheritance which she and her husband hold on the day of the said husband's death, and she may stay in

---

[111] *CEC*, no. 321, cf. no. 170, with commentary by Barraclough on pp. 322-33.

her husband's house for forty days after his death, within which period her dower will be assigned to her.

No widow will be compelled to marry so long as she wishes to live without a husband, provided that she give security that she will not marry without our consent if she shall hold of us, or without the consent of the lord of whom she holds, if she shall hold of another.

If anyone holding a lay fief of us dies, and our sheriff or bailiff shows our letters patent of summons for a debt which the deceased owed to us, the sheriff or our bailiff will be allowed to attach and list the chattels of the deceased found in lay fee to the value of that debt, by the view of lawful men, so that nothing is removed until the evident debt is paid to us, and the residue will be relinquished to the executors to carry out the will of the deceased. And if he owes us nothing, all the chattels will be accounted as the deceased's, saving their reasonable shares to his wife and children.

At national level, the root of the problem lay in baronial resentment at what they perceived as abuses of the king's power to intervene as their overlord in the succession to their estates. At Runnymede, the barons did not challenge the king's right to take a relief from those inheriting estates held from him, but managed to secure fixed maximum payments. They had no issue with the king's entitlement to find marriage-partners for heirs (male or female) in his wardship[112] - an excellent source of patronage for royal favourites including those willing to pay heavily for the privilege - but were promised that the marriages would be to partners of suitable social standing after next of kin had been informed. They accepted that widows could not retain their late husbands' estates indefinitely and

---

[112] Wardship was the temporary custody by the lord of the person and estates of a tenant who had succeeded as a minor. It ceased once the tenant came of age.

could not go on to remarry whomsoever they wished; but they obtained guarantees that these women could keep the portions to which they were entitled, would not be put out of their homes for forty days, and would not be remarried against their will. They also secured protection for the chattels of the deceased, against excessive claims ostensibly for repayment of debts.[113]

As we discussed at the start, King John had been notorious for exploiting his rights in this area. In 1214, for example, he had charged William fitz Alan £6,666 13s. 4d. for succession to the family barony and Margaret widow of Robert de Clavering £1,000 for (among other items) freedom not to remarry.[114] But these were far from being novel causes of friction between a king and his barons. In his coronation charter of August 1100, John's great-grandfather Henry I had promised to charge only a 'just and lawful relief', to take advice before giving the daughters of deceased tenants in marriage, to guarantee to widows the lands to which they were entitled, to refrain from forcing them into remarriage, and to impose limits on loss of chattels.[115] Yet it did not stop him taking advantage of his position to boost his coffers. To cite only one example from the exchequer pipe roll of 1130, Ranulf III's great-grandmother the Countess Lucy was recorded as owing £100 'for her father's land' in Lincolnshire (to add to £166 13s. 4d. already paid) plus a further £333, 6s. 8d. 'so that she need not marry within five years'.[116] Heavy reliefs and other payments

---

[113] See e.g. McKechnie, *Magna Carta: a Commentary*, pp. 196-203, 212-21, 321-29.

[114] Holt, *Magna Carta*, pp. 190-91.

[115] *EHD*, II, no. 19.

[116] *Great Roll of the Pipe for the Thirty First Year of the Reign of King Henry I*, ed. J.A. Green (Pipe Roll Society, London, 2012), p. 87. For discussion of Lucy's position, see P. Dalton, 'Aiming at the Impossible: Ranulf II earl of Chester and Lincolnshire in the Reign of King Stephen' in Thacker, ed., *Earldom of Chester and its Charters*, pp. 109-34, at p. 110, and J.A. Green, *The Aristocracy of Norman England* (Cambridge, 1997), pp 368-71.

of this nature, apparently unrelated to any fixed tariff, continued to be levied by the crown through the second half of the twelfth century.[117]

By the 1180s, the relief payable for succession to a holding on the part of an under-tenant (not one holding directly of the king) had become fixed by custom at 100 shillings per knight's fee: in other words, £5 multiplied by however many knights' military service to the lord was due from the property. The equivalent sums due from barons as tenants-in-chief of the king were acknowledged to be at the latter's discretion - hence the exorbitant amounts levied by John and his predecessors - but there are also indications that £100 per 'barony' (i.e. £100 for the baron's full estate) was by then coming to be seen as a reasonable figure.[118] These sums were duly enshrined in clause 2 of the Runnymede Magna Carta. The fact that, along with issues affecting under-age heirs and widows, fixed reliefs were dealt with so early in the document - as they were in drafts such as the Articles of the Barons - suggests that they were very high on the list of priorities for those who opposed King John. But how does all this compare with the way these matters were handled in Cheshire?

We know that Earl Ranulf exercised his right to find marriage-partners for his wards. Probably in the early 1190s, he gave Helen, the heiress to Cheadle, to be wife of Geoffrey de Dutton, a youngest son for whom this was presumably an entry into landed

---

[117] E.g. W.L. Warren, *Henry II* (London, 1973), pp. 385-86; Holt, *Magna Carta*, pp. 183-85; G.J. White, *Restoration and Reform: Recovery from Civil War in England, 1153-1165* (Cambridge, 2000), p. 105, n. 154.

[118] *Glanvill*, ed. Hall, p. 108; *Dialogus de Scaccario*, ed. Johnson *et al.*, p. 121, cf. p. 94, where £100 is given as an illustrative figure for the 'relief' on a barony; cf. also McKechnie, *Magna Carta: a Commentary*, pp. 197-98, which cites the pipe roll of 1198-99 as describing £100 for a barony as a 'reasonable relief'. Note, however, the cautionary words on how far this figure had been accepted in J. Hudson, 'Magna Carta, the *ius commune*, and the English Common Law' in Loengard, ed., *Magna Carta and the England of King John*, pp. 99-119, at p. 113.

society.[119] We cannot say, however, whether any charges levied, to claim custody of one's relatives, to obtain a bride (or groom) or to avoid an unwilling marriage, were thought to be excessive; in 1182-83 Elias de Swettenham paid 'for custody of his nephews', thereby ensuring that wardship and control of the future destiny of their lands would remain within the family, and might well have thought the fairly modest sum of 20 shillings (£1) he parted with to be money well spent.[120] As for reliefs, such figures as we have suggest that 'reasonable' sums were already being charged. In 1180-81 William fitz Richard paid £10 as the relief for two knights' fees, and in 1183-84 Ralf fitz Simon accounted for £15 as the relief for three, precisely the rates laid down both at Runnymede and in the Cheshire Magna Carta.[121] A charge of £100 in the early 1190s to David de Malpas for the right to hold the barony of Malpas until the previous holder's heirs reimbursed him has the appearance of a relief on the scale for baronies acknowledged at Runnymede, but this followed seven years in which the estate had been in the earl's hands after being forfeited for failure to do service, so it cannot be taken as typical.[122]

All things considered, grievances over reliefs, under-age heirs and widows seem to have been less of an issue in Cheshire than in the

---

[119] CEC, no. 261.

[120] Cheshire in the Pipe Rolls, 1158-1301, ed. R. Stewart-Brown (Record Society of Lancashire and Cheshire, XCII, 1938), p. 9.

[121] Cheshire in the Pipe Rolls, ed. Stewart-Brown, pp. 7, 10. There is the possible objection to the evidence in both this and the preceding footnote that it relates to a period when Cheshire was temporarily in the king's hands during the minority of Ranulf III and that 'normal' levies might not have been imposed at that time. However, Dialogus de Scaccario, ed. Johnson et al., p. 121, is clear that in the case of a holding which is part of an estate 'fallen into the king's hands for want of an heir or otherwise, the inheritor will only pay the king as relief what he would have had to pay to his own lord, namely, a hundred shillings for each knight's fee' (i.e. reliefs would be at the usual rate and that rate was £5 per knight's fee, as in the Cheshire examples).

[122] CEC, no. 266.

68

rest of the kingdom. The same is probably true of the safeguarding of legacies against excessive claims for debt, since this occupies only a brief sentence at the end of the clause - lacking any elaboration of the issue - compared to the space devoted to the topic in clause 26 at Runnymede. The problems were dealt with half way through the charter, not almost at the beginning, they were covered more succinctly, and the substance of Magna Carta clauses 3-5, on wardship, were omitted altogether. The absence from the Cheshire charter of any reference to £100 as the maximum relief for a barony also suggests that, in practice, this was not an area of concern: the figure was conventionally associated with the king's immediate tenants, not the earl's, and since - as we have seen - no Cheshire barony exceeded ten knights' fees[123] it was more important to their holders to secure the rate of £5 per fee. In this they succeeded, since this was still the rate observed in the fourteenth century.[124] These issues were, of course, too important generally for the Cheshire barons to ignore them altogether when seeking guarantees from their earl to match those granted by the king. But it would be wrong to conclude from the presence of this clause within the Cheshire Magna Carta that Ranulf III was seen as tarred with the same brush as King John.

Clause 9

The statement that 'town air makes free' was coined in the nineteenth century and is not an accurate rendering of medieval law and custom. However, the statement has at least popularised the notion that residence in a medieval town could lead to release from unfree status - the issue at the heart of this clause. Defining 'towns', however, is less than straightforward, since there are both economic and constitutional criteria. Some flourishing commercial centres, such as Towcester,

---

[123] *Calendar of Court Rolls of Chester*, ed. Stewart-Brown, pp. xlvi-xlvii.

[124] *Accounts of the County of Chester*, ed. Stewart-Brown, pp. 17, 39, 152, 204 (the last a case in 1350-51 where relief on one-third of two-thirds of half a knight's fee was calculated on the basis of £5 per fee down to the last one-twelfth of a penny).

continued throughout the Middle Ages to be governed by their lords of the manor, while tiny places like Stanstead Abbots already had 'burgesses' indicative of privileged status at the time of Domesday Book. It was those towns which enjoyed a measure of autonomy - as 'boroughs' inhabited by 'burgesses' who held 'burgages' - which were seen as communities of the free.[125]

Medieval Chester was certainly a town by any criterion: self-governed by twelve judges on the evidence of Domesday Book and with 'a harbour for ships coming from Aquitaine, Spain, Ireland and Germany, which … come and unload at the city bay with many goods' according to the local monk Lucian just over a century later.[126] By then, Henry II's acquisitions in Ireland had undoubtedly increased Chester's prosperity and strategic importance and it doubled its population to remain a town in the 'second rank' between the eleventh and sixteenth centuries. At the time of Magna Carta Chester probably housed between 3,000 and 4,000 people. Like many towns, its growth was faster than that of the country as a whole and must have been achieved partly through inward migration.[127] The freedom enjoyed by members of the urban community is evident from charters issued by Ranulf III detailing their liberties. None specifically mentions the liberation of incoming villeins but the free status of 'citizens' (Latin: *cives*) is evident from the various protections guaranteed to their chattels; those of a villein belonged to his lord.[128] In such circumstances, it is hardly surprising that the Cheshire barons showed a similar concern about the departure of their villeins to Chester as they did about losing them to the earl's jurisdiction.

---

[125] S. Reynolds, *An Introduction to the History of English Towns* (Oxford, 1977), pp. 98-102; White, *Medieval English Landscape*, pp. 100-101, 116-18.

[126] *Domesday Book: Cheshire*, ed. Morgan, 262 c, d; *Liber Luciani de Laude Cestrie*, ed. Taylor, p. 46, cited in D.M. Palliser, ed., *Chester, 1066-1971: Contemporary Descriptions by Residents and Visitors* (Chester, 1972), p. 6.

[127] *VCH: Cheshire*, V, pt. 2 (2005), pp. 3-4.

[128] *CEC*, nos. 256, 257, 258.

Across most of England, as population rose through the twelfth and thirteenth centuries, some movement from an increasingly-pressurised countryside into the towns was generally welcomed, including by many lords of rural manors disinclined to chase up villeins who were surplus to requirements in any case. Nevertheless, there was a presumption that a lord had a year and a day to reclaim a villein who had taken up residence in a borough if he wished to do so. This entitlement can be traced back to Henry I's reign, among the customs of Newcastle-upon-Tyne, which had laid down that 'if anyone has held land in burgage for a year and a day justly and without challenge he need not answer any claimant' and had added the following:

> If a villein come to reside in the borough, and shall remain as a burgess in the borough for a year and a day, he shall thereafter always remain there, unless there was a previous agreement between him and his lord for him to remain there for a certain time.[129]

Similar provisions had since been made for several other boroughs, among them Pembroke, Lincoln and Nottingham.[130] Legal opinion under Henry II was that:

> If any villein stays peaceably for a year and a day in a privileged town and is admitted as a citizen into their commune, that is to say their gild, he is thereby freed from villeinage.[131]

These phrases leave room for interpretation over how exactly a villein gained public admission to the urban community and so

---

[129] *EHD*, II, no. 298.
[130] A. Ballard, *British Borough Charters, 1042-1216* (Cambridge, 1913), pp. 103-105.
[131] *Glanvill*, ed. Hall, p. 58; cf. Reynolds, *English Medieval Towns*, pp. 100-101.

(metaphorically) started the clock ticking, but the image of the borough as a place where enterprising villeins and their families could build a new life - with some prospect that their lord would be either unable or unwilling to frustrate them - is clear enough.

Cheshire, however, differed from most English counties in being - by the standards of the time - significantly under-populated. The relevant clause in Ranulf III's charter was drafted in terms which saw the freedom to be gained by dwelling in Chester not as opportunity but as threat; it was another demonstration of the barons' reluctance to lose control of the villeins cultivating their estates. We do not know whether there had been any cases in Chester of villeins being recognised as 'burgesses' or 'citizens' in under twelve months, but the barons' concern seems to have been to ensure that local practice would at least conform to that of the rest of the kingdom: that they would have a full year and a day to claim back their villeins. It was not an issue which exercised the negotiators at Runnymede and there is no comparable clause in King John's Magna Carta. Nor was there any mention of the other Cheshire towns which Ranulf III recognised as boroughs, Frodsham and Macclesfield, among which the former had almost certainly received its charter by this time.[132] It is impossible to say why this was the case. Perhaps Chester was such a magnet, compared with the others, that it was the only one where the barons had any concern about loss of their villeins. Alternatively, the earl may have silently declined to extend the clause to the other boroughs, since these were seen as enterprises to which he was eager to attract new settlement.

Clause 10

This clause was concerned to impose limits on liability to military service. At Runnymede, there was a vague undertaking in clause 16 not to extract excessive service:

---

[132] *CEC*, no. 371; *Calendar of Court Rolls of Chester*, ed. Stewart-Brown, p. 243; Ballard, *British Borough Charters,* p. xxxvi.

No man will be compelled to perform more service for a knight's fee or for any other free tenement than is due therefrom.

There were also some provisions relating to castle guard, the system whereby knights supplied garrisons for the castles of their lords (clause 29):

No constable is to compel any knight to give money for castle guard, if he is willing to perform that guard in his own person or by another reliable man, if for some good reason he is unable to do it himself, and if we take or send him on military service, he will be excused the guard in proportion to the period of his service in our army.

The Cheshire charter took up these themes with a series of promises about when and where military service could be required, going into a level of detail which reflected the county's position in an often-hostile frontier zone. If we are right to assign the issue of the charter to a period when civil war was looming, it was also the product of the anxieties of earl and barons alike to define what loyal service would actually involve.

The first matter dealt with was the restriction of service to 'home' territory. Resistance to having to fight overseas had fuelled the hostility of the northern barons to King John during 1213 and six of them had refused to sail with him on campaign to Poitou the following February. After he had returned to England, defeated, in October 1214, the issue would surface in the so-called 'Unknown Charter of Liberties', thought to represent a preliminary stage in negotiations during the early months of 1215; this included a concession that the king's men did not have to go with the army outside England, other than to Normandy or Brittany. In the event, this particular promise featured neither in the Runnymede Magna Carta nor in the 'Articles of the Barons', the draft which preceded it, and it looks as if the king and his advisors managed to negotiate its omission. However, the

73

underlying concern would become a recurring theme among the nobility of thirteenth-century Europe. The Golden Bull of Hungary in 1222, for example, granted under duress by King Andrew II as a statement of baronial and clerical rights and privileges, limited the obligation to serve outside the realm to counts and paid knights.[133]

As for Cheshire, the issue was interpreted in a way which reaffirmed the county's distinctiveness from the rest of the kingdom. Ranulf's barons did of course owe the earl military service wherever required for knights' fees held from him elsewhere in England; this lay behind the provisions in a charter issued by the next earl, John le Scot, in favour of the constable John de Lacy, which specifically described the fees in question as 'in England' rather than in Cheshire.[134] But in securing a promise that, for their Cheshire holdings, they would not have to provide military service to the earl 'beyond the Lyme', other than voluntarily and at his own expense, the barons were asserting their responsibilities to fight as necessary within the county but not elsewhere; the specific justification was 'the heavy service they give in Cheshire'.[135]

---

[133] I.J. Sanders, *Feudal Military Service in England* (Oxford, 1956), pp. 52-58; Holt, *The Northerners*, pp. 91-92 (which notes that 'cornage' tenure which was widespread in Cumberland was associated with military service around and beyond the Scottish border but not elsewhere); Holt, *Magna Carta*, pp. 77-78, 239-40, 418-28.

[134] *CEC*, no. 440. Cf. W. Farrer, ed., *Honors and Knights' Fees* (Manchester, 1923-25), II, pp. 111-12, where the hereditary steward of Chester owed the service of being the first in the earl's army going to Wales and the last in returning in respect of his tenure of Harmston (Lincolnshire), not on account of any Cheshire lands. Cf. also *CEC*, no. 315 (probably to be dated 1211-12), which shows the canons of Trentham (Staffordshire) being released from their previous obligation to provide a footsoldier for service in Wales.

[135] In 1211-12 knights of the honour of Hastings had asserted that they owed no military service outside the rape (district) of Hastings except at their lord's expense (Sanders, *Feudal Military Service* , p. 55); this was another area

The slope in the background is the western edge of the Lyme, as seen today from Moss Hall aqueduct on the Shropshire Union canal, half a mile north-west of Audlem ('old Lyme'). The River Weaver, in the foreground, soon turns left to run northwards along the base of the scarp.

The Lyme, a district over 50 miles long marking the county's eastern and south-eastern border with Derbyshire, Staffordshire and - in part - with Lancashire and Shropshire as well, covered all the routes to the earl of Chester's Midlands estates, as well as those to London. As a sharply-defined upland area of woods and moors, it may well have been a political and administrative boundary in Roman and post-Roman times before coming to delineate the edges of Cheshire in the

which could claim a particular defensive role, namely against invasion from the English Channel.

75

tenth century.[136] Consciousness of its significance in separating the county from England as a whole was deep-rooted. All the land which Robert fitz Nigel held 'in Cheshire within Lyme' was forfeited to the earl, apparently in 1185 at a time when Ranulf was a ward of the king. A decade later the monk Lucian specifically mentioned it as the boundary between 'the province of Chester' and the rest of the country. In or shortly before 1214, Aenora Malbank, a coheiress to the barony of Nantwich, conveyed to Henry de Audley all her lands 'in Cheshire within Lyme'.[137] And at an unknown date - possibly the early- to mid-1220s when he was at odds with Henry III's government - Earl Ranulf (notwithstanding the concession in clause 6 of his great charter) prohibited the 'men of Lyme' from asserting their woods, because the clearances would reduce its effectiveness as a defensive barrier.[138]

Although the Lyme was the only county boundary mentioned, the charter was formally interpreted as exempting the barons from military obligations outside Cheshire in any direction.[139] An inquest into service due from Cheshire 'in time of war with Wales', dated 11 May 1288 - by which time the earldom was of course in the hands of

---

[136] J. McN. Dodgson, ed., *The Place-Names of Cheshire*, I (Cambridge, 1970), pp. 2-6; Higham, *Origins of Cheshire*, pp. 95-96, 120; R. Coates, 'The Lyme', *Journal of English Place-Name Society*, XXXVI (2004), pp. 39–50. Higham's map (p. 120) helpfully emphasises place-names such as Ashton-under-Lyne and Lyme Hall in the north, and Newcastle-under-Lyme and Audlem further south, as broadly indicative of the Lyme as a Cheshire boundary.

[137] *CEC*, nos. 266, 395; *Liber Luciani de Laude Cestrie*, ed. Taylor, p. 65.

[138] Barraclough, 'Earldom and County Palatine', pp. 52-53, 56-57. For contemporary references to the Lyme as a boundary to south Lancashire, see J. Tait, *Medieval Manchester and the Beginnings of Lancashire* (Manchester, 1904), pp. 12, 138, 180, 193.

[139] For this purpose, the western boundary of Cheshire was being interpreted as the River Clwyd by the mid-fourteenth century (see the claims of Henry duke of Lancaster, died 1361, in the penultimate paragraph below: Ormerod, *History of the County Palatine*, 1882, I, p. 705).

the crown - specified that knights and infantry should be provided 'within the bounds of Cheshire … according to the tenor of the great common charter of Cheshire'; 'and if any army should come from elsewhere into Cheshire, or if [Chester] castle should be besieged' each landholder owing service for knights' fees should 'come at the king's summons with all his force to drive away the same according to the tenor of the common charter aforesaid'. In practice, however, Edward I came to rely heavily on troops from Cheshire for his Welsh and Scottish campaigns and seems to have had little difficulty in overcoming any restrictions which the charter implied: sometimes acknowledging that the county's contribution graciously went beyond its obligations, sometimes not. In 1300, for example, troops from Cheshire did not begin to be paid by the king until they had mustered along with those from elsewhere in the country at Carlisle.[140] Just as King John had evidently declined to yield on the issue of 'service abroad' at Runnymede, so - in practice, and in a Cheshire context - did his grandson.

The rest of the clause addressed at some length the issue of castle guard (or ward), the obligation to provide a garrison for Chester castle. At this point, as we observed in the commentary on the introductory section of the charter, there is actually a departure from the usual exclusive focus on Cheshire, since the obligation is portrayed as incumbent upon the knights of the honour of Chester across the rest of the kingdom - the earl's 'knights from England' as they are described, estimated to number about 170 in comparison to the 80 or so in Cheshire itself. The castle is seen here in its role as the *caput* (head) of the honour as a whole, not merely as an administrative headquarters for the county. That said, the issue was still of acute interest to the barons of Cheshire, partly on account of their holdings outside the county and partly because of their obligations in an emergency. Forty days' service was a typical length for castle guard, supposedly fulfilled as part of an annual rota; we know, for example,

---

[140] *Calendar of Court Rolls of Chester*, ed. Stewart-Brown, pp. liii-lvi, 109-16; Morgan, *War and Society*, pp. 29-31.

that Henry II's sheriff and justice Bertram de Verdun, who was entrusted with the administration of the honour during Ranulf III's minority, was expected to find one knight for 40 days at Chester castle in respect of a tenancy from the earl near Leek in Staffordshire.[141]

In practice - as happened elsewhere, hence Magna Carta clause 29 - we may presume that this service was often commuted to a money payment which could be used to pay men-at-arms hired for as long as necessary.[142] But whether commuted or not, Ranulf's barons, and by extension their knights, were specifically exempt of such castle guard duties in respect of their holdings in Cheshire if the county was at peace. Only if it was threatened with attack or the castle was under siege must they answer the earl's summons, and then only for as long as was necessary to repel the assault. Other 'services' due to the earl, such as the reliefs and court-attendances described in previous clauses, were of course safeguarded.

As we have seen, the obligations incumbent upon the Cheshire barons in the event of an invasion of the county were described in the Inquest of 1288 as being in accordance with Ranulf III's great charter. The statements in the Inquest that, for each knight's fee held from the earl, a baron had to supply 'one horse fully-armed or two unarmed ... with all his footmen holding forinsec land within the said fees' were not actually in the charter but appear to represent the customs it was intended to uphold. On the one hand, the expectation was to provide, for each knight's fee, either one fully-armed knight or two horses with unarmed (or lesser-armed) riders; on the other, it was to supply infantry drawn from (or provided by) freeholding under-tenants, often holders of fractions of a manor or

---

[141] *Calendar of Court Rolls of Chester*, ed. Stewart-Brown, pp. liii-liv; Farrer, *Honors and Knights' Fees*, II, p. 255.
[142] *Cheshire in the Pipe Rolls*, ed. Stewart-Brown, p. 17; J.S. Moore, 'Anglo-Norman Garrisons', *Anglo-Norman Studies XXII* (Woodbridge, 2000), pp. 205-75; S. Painter, 'Castle Guard' in R. Liddiard, ed., *Anglo-Norman Castles* (Woodbridge, 2003), pp. 203-10.

vill, who would normally offer rent or various duties to their immediate lords but who had still had a residual obligation of 'forinsec' ('external') service to the earl as overlord.[143] This would include the requirement to come to the common defence of the county in time of emergency, doubtless protected by the haubergeon and mail already referred to in clause 3. Such service seems to have been regarded as customary unless specifically rescinded, as happened to land at Acton in the 1190s held by the monks of Stanlaw from Richard of Aston apparently for a term of 30 years; Earl Ranulf notified his justiciar of Chester that he had freed the monks of the forinsec service they owed him for this land.[144]

Yet - to revisit the point made in connection with the limitation on fighting beyond the borders of Cheshire - the tenor of this clause is liable to give a misleading impression that there was a grudging attitude to armed conflict within the county. Thirteenth-century Cheshire has rightly been described as 'a highly militarised society' and it remained so for the rest of the Middle Ages. By Ranulf III's time, the barons, along with the knights and freeholders who held from them, had several generations' experience of actual or threatened fighting against the Welsh; they wanted guaranteed limits on their obligations but it was as much in their interests as those of the earl to defend the county and its major castle. It was a county which welcomed outlaws from the rest of the kingdom, at least partly because of their potential as soldiers, and where the terms of land tenure could be unusually specific: thus, in 1301, William Helsby was holding Helsby from Richard fitz Alan, earl of Arundel, for the service of a horseman with armour for 40 days in time of war, while Richard Brown's tenancy from fitz Alan was for the service for 40 days of a man with a bow and a quiverful of arrows. The sense of preparedness for war meant that troops could readily be assembled; this certainly contributed - alongside geographical convenience - to

---

[143] *Calendar of Court Rolls of Chester*, ed. Stewart-Brown, pp. lv-lvi, 112-13; Pollock and Maitland, *History of English Law*, I, pp. 238-39, 244-45, 277-78.
[144] *CEC*, no. 210.

the fact that (if estimates are correct) some 10-15% of the adult male population of Cheshire fought in one or more of Edward I's campaigns.[145] That in turn helped to establish a tradition of the crown looking to Cheshire for soldiers in the fourteenth and fifteenth centuries: unhindered by a charter which had imposed checks on what could be demanded as feudal obligations but had not set any limits on what could be contracted for in return for money.

Clause 11

The last clause in which Earl Ranulf made any specific concessions related to his itinerant serjeants. These were armed police officers who were expected to ride around the county keeping the peace: seemingly a counterpart for the shire as a whole of the foresters who policed the forests.[146] Other than in wartime, the number of serjeants was to be restricted from hereon to twelve and curbs were placed on their entitlement to be supplied with food free of charge. The rather awkward phraseology suggests that they could still help themselves to whatever was already in a house but would have to pay for any further supplies. Additionally, the barons as a whole were to be exempt of any obligation to feed the serjeants from their demesne lands (those they had not leased out). Even finding provender for the master serjeant's horse in the summer half of the year was to be voluntary. If war broke out, more serjeants could be deployed by the earl but only after consultation with his barons.

Clause 28 of Magna Carta demonstrates resentment across the country against the practice of royal officials taking provisions without payment:

---

[145] Morgan, *War and Society*, pp. 31-37 (quotation on p. 37).
[146] Crouch, 'Administration', p. 90; Stewart-Brown, *Serjeants of the Peace,* pp. 3-25.

No constable or any other of our bailiffs will take any man's corn or other chattels unless he pays cash for them at once or can delay payment with the agreement of the seller.

Customary levies of 'sheaves and offerings' by the earl's serjeants and other officials (described as beadles) had already featured in clause 5 of the Cheshire charter. The particular grievance addressed here in clause 11 seems to have been that there was currently no limit either to the number of serjeants who could be engaged or to the extent to which they could demand to be fed. The issue was complicated by the fact that - to judge from claims made in the following century - the barons had their own 'serjeants of the peace' patrolling their estates with entitlement to be fed on demand:[147] a situation which - as we saw in clause 1 - must have led to confrontations over who should arrest criminals, quite apart from the double burden on those expected to give them free food. Compounding the grievance was Ranulf's readiness - in this respect as in others - to use release from the imposition as a source of patronage. Sometime between 1194 and 1208 he exempted the monks of Chester abbey from having to feed his serjeants from any of their lands in Wirral, other than six foresters on foot; the abbey's demesne manors of Sutton, Eastham, Bromborough and Irby were spared even this imposition. The same charter went on to say that, in a wartime emergency, the number of serjeants might be increased and they might have to be fed, but even then the four manors would be exempt.[148] The monks of Stanlaw, in respect of their holding at Willington, and Peter the clerk, for that of Thornton-le-Moors, were others freed of any obligation to feed the earl's serjeants and foresters.[149] There seems little doubt, as we argued with the 'forest' clause, no. 6, that some genuine complaints about current practice were being addressed here, encouraged by the idea

---

[147] Ormerod, *History of the County Palatine* (1882), I, pp. 526, 704; Stewart-Brown, *Serjeants of the Peace*, pp. 19-22.
[148] *CEC*, no. 230.
[149] *CEC*, nos. 215, 285.

that if the earl could make concessions for those in his special favour, he ought to do the same for his barons as a whole.

There are glimpses of how all this worked out in the pipe rolls and in the Inquest of Service of 1288. In 1241, the year of Henry III's invasion of Wales, the number of serjeants was put as high as 36; later in the 1240s, still a period of conflict with the Welsh, there appear to have been over 20; the Inquest of 1288 - explicitly covering arrangements 'in time of war' - mentions twelve serjeants plus a further eight in the hundred of Macclesfield. A wartime increase in the complement of serjeants was of course provided for in Earl Ranulf's charter but the Inquest offers some other signs of the respect in which the charter was held. The single mounted serjeant was entitled to free fodder for his horse but only during the winter months and not from the barons' own demesnes: its supply was a 'forinsec' obligation, which (as in the discussion of the previous clause) presumably meant on lands leased by the barons to their tenants. Otherwise, the serjeants were to 'keep the peace ... at their own charges' unless they went outside the county.[150] Although Ranulf's great charter was not mentioned, much of this could have come straight out of clause 11. It had evidently succeeded in easing the burden which these roving officers inflicted on the community at large.[151]

Clause 12

The next clause was one for which there was no precedent in the Runnymede Magna Carta. We have seen that John had not actually

---

[150] *Cheshire in the Pipe Rolls*, ed. Stewart-Brown, pp. 67, 69, 77, 88, 95 (cf. p. 119 for the bounty received by the serjeants of one shilling for the head of each captured thief); *Calendar of Court Rolls of Chester*, ed. Stewart-Brown, pp. 111, 115 (cf. p. 141 for the serjeants in trouble for not declaring booty found on a body and p. 232 for a case in which John the serjeant was wounded when trying to apprehend Gilbert son of the Cook at Titherington).
[151] Even so, several individuals were indicted at Macclesfield in 1290 for failure to feed the forest serjeants and their dogs (*Calendar of Court Rolls of Chester*, ed. Stewart-Brown, p. 245).

conceded everything that the barons wanted - their wish for a ban on military service overseas being a prime example - but the king had not drawn attention to this in the document. Earl Ranulf, by contrast, seems to have been eager to stress his freedom to reject as well as to accept his barons' demands and the petitions they had 'remitted' were duly itemised here. All related to what elsewhere in the country would have been deemed 'regalian rights' - the king's customary entitlements to wreck, the control of forests and the profits of local law-courts, enjoyed here by the earl of Chester instead. But while he chose not to divest himself of these rights, Earl Ranulf did leave open the possibility that they might be granted away 'by my grace and mercy', as a special favour to those in receipt of patronage at some point in the future.

Roger de Montalt, the earl's hereditary steward, appears to have been denied the right to take possession of whatever the sea washed up onto his land, specified here as wreck and fish. Many lords of coastal estates had in fact established this entitlement, in place of the crown, by the thirteenth century,[152] and as the 'baron of Mold' with holdings south and west of the Dee estuary Roger could certainly have profited from mishaps to shipping using the port of Chester. Unless the reference in the charter is to some minor modification of the custom, it looks as if the earl was asserting a clear determination to retain the right for himself.

---

[152] S.A. Moore, *A History of the Foreshore* (London, 1888), pp. 1-68. As an example, back in Henry I's reign, the abbot of Ramsey had proved his entitlements in respect of Brancaster (Norfolk) by reference in the shire court to past cases of taking stranded whales and a barrel of wine: *English Lawsuits*, I, no. 256. The hospital at Denhall, on the Wirral side of the Dee estuary, later claimed the right of wreck (*VCH: Cheshire*, III, 1980, p. 185); Henry duke of Lancaster (died 1361), who as baron of Halton held lands along the River Mersey, also cited wreck among his customary entitlements (Ormerod, *History of the County Palatine*, 1882, I, p. 703).

The steward also failed to secure some further forest concessions. He apparently sought the liberty of 'hunting with dogs' - an offence duly prosecuted at Macclesfield in the 1280s[153] - and also ventured without success into the more stylised bloodsports associated with parks, which were managed enclosures within the forests. In company with un-named 'others', he petitioned regarding the shooting of a fixed number of arrows at deer driven towards a target-area; the 'others' also seem to have been keen to watch hounds chase hares along a prepared course. It is not clear whether the petitioners were seeking some extension or deregulation of this activity, but the implication is that they were hoping to have some sport laid on whenever the earl summoned them to Chester![154] If so, they were disappointed.

Some perceived inequity may have lain behind the petition regarding agistment of swine in the forest, the customary entitlement to grazing rights in return for payment; various anomalies in Delamere forest, for example, whereby certain vills paid in pigs, others in pence, whether or not there were any acorns available, are apparent from fourteenth-century account rolls.[155] It is worth noting, however, that animal feeding rights in the earl's forests were another of the matters which Ranulf was prepared to use as a means of patronage,[156] so we may simply be looking here at a failed attempt to extend favours from the few to the many.

---

[153] *Calendar of Court Rolls of Chester*, ed. Stewart-Brown, pp. 222, 226-27, 232, 244.

[154] S.A. Mileson, *Parks in Medieval England* (Oxford, 2009), pp. 28-32; O.H. Creighton, *Designs upon the Land: Elite Landscapes of the Middle Ages* (Woodbridge, 2009), pp. 152-53; and on the subject generally, R. Liddiard, ed., *The Medieval Park: New Perspectives* (Macclesfield, 2007).

[155] *Accounts of the County of Chester*, ed. Stewart-Brown, pp. xx, 3, 17, 35, 71, 77, 91.

[156] *CEC*, nos. 285, 408, 434.

As for the 'laws in Wich', these were set out in detail in Domesday Book as applicable within the designated confines of the salt-making towns of Northwich, Nantwich and Middlewich. Among them was the statement that:

Anyone who incurred a penalty within these boundaries could pay a fine of 2 shillings or of 30 boilings of salt, except for homicide, or for a theft for which a thief was condemned to death. Those who committed such offences were punished as in the rest of the shire.

'Thirty boilings of salt' - a reference to the medieval method of salt-production by boiling brine - was deemed equivalent to two packloads of salt.[157]

It is not clear from the phraseology in the Cheshire charter whether the rejected petition 'for the amercement of the judges of Wich' related to penalties imposed upon them - presumably for non-attendance as in clause 5, where the sum of two shillings is precisely that deemed equivalent to 30 boilings of salt - or to penalties imposed by them or as a result of their judgments. Tait thought the former, suggesting that a reduction in the standard amercement was being sought.[158] This may be so, but Ranulf's refusal to change the 'laws in Wich' implies that more than this was at stake. As Domesday Book makes clear, in the passage just quoted, the duties of the judges in the salt-making towns did not extend to the earl's 'pleas of the sword', but for the lesser offences within their jurisdiction there was evidently a fixed penalty, which could be paid in kind. There may well have been a wish to amend or abolish this penalty, possibly for no other reason than that it was thought too inflexible. For his part, the earl - who

---

[157] *Domesday Book: Cheshire*, ed. Morgan, 268 a, b.
[158] *Chartulary of St Werburgh, Chester*, ed, Tait, I, p. 102.

derived an income from the profits of the 'Wich' courts[159] - was obviously unwilling to end the arrangement.

What these rejected petitions appear to have had in common is that they largely related to the local circumstances of particular individuals or communities, rather than covering issues of great moment to the Cheshire barons and their tenants as a whole. This was doubtless a reason why Ranulf felt confident in turning them down.

Clause 13

This concluding clause tied the earl of Chester's great charter very closely to that of the king. It insisted that the liberties which had been granted should apply not only to the barons and those who held directly from the earl but also to the 'knights and free tenants of the whole of Cheshire', whoever their immediate lord might be. Strictly speaking, this conflicted with the statement in clause 11 to the effect that the barons' demesnes were to be exempt from feeding the earl's serjeants but land held by their tenants would not be. But the overall sense was that the county community at large - all freeholders, though not the unfree - should benefit from the earl's concessions, which were binding on himself and his heirs to come.

Magna Carta had said much the same thing. In clause 1, the king had 'granted to all the free men of our realm for ourselves and our heirs for ever, all the liberties written below'. Clause 60, quoted earlier in this discussion, had provided for the king's own tenants-in-chief to pass on to those who held from them the same benefits as they had received. The last clause, no. 63, had repeated the king's wish that 'the men in our realm will have and hold all the aforesaid liberties ... for themselves and their heirs of us and our heirs in all things and places for ever'. None of this phraseology is close enough to that of the Cheshire Magna Carta to suggest that one is a direct copy of the

---

[159] *Accounts of the County of Chester*, ed. Stewart-Brown, pp. 144 (Northwich), 146 (Middlewich), 174 (Nantwich).

other; indeed, clause 13 of the Cheshire charter, in stressing that it is the earl who grants these liberties to the county's knights and free tenants, may have been deliberately departing from Runnymede's clause 60, which implies a devolution to the barons of responsibility for passing on the benefits they had received. But whatever the precise significance of the wording, the same general idea features in both documents: the barons should observe the liberties they had been granted in their dealings with their own tenants and freeholders, and in so doing they would ensure that the concessions were applicable to the whole community. This can hardly be coincidence. It reinforces the argument that the barons of Cheshire, in seeking a charter of liberties from their earl, and the earl of Chester, in agreeing to grant one, were consciously creating what they saw as a local equivalent of the Runnymede Magna Carta: addressing the issues of particular relevance to the county and reasserting its communal independence from the rest of the kingdom.

Witnesses

The Runnymede Magna Carta had not included a witness list at the end but had referred back, as witnesses, to those loyal clergy and lay barons named as the king's advisors in the introduction. The reissue of 1216 would adopt the same practice. Earl Ranulf's great charter, by contrast, concluded by naming 29 men as witnesses, adding 'the whole county of Chester' presumably to embrace all those present at the relevant county court in Chester castle. Hugh abbot of Chester, who headed the list, was more usually found witnessing charters in favour of ecclesiastical beneficiaries,[160] but he lent weight to the document, as he would seven years later to the formal agreement over the marriage of Ranulf's heir to the daughter of the ruler of Gwynedd.[161] Apart from him, the witnesses seem to have been drawn from the earl's administrative and household service, from the junior

---

[160] *CEC*, nos. 248, 335, 359-60, 378, 382-83, 386-89, but cf. nos. 258, 285, 357, 409.
[161] *CEC*, no. 411; Hugh Grylle was abbot of Chester from 1208 to 1226.

ranks of Cheshire baronial families, or from minor landholders, whether tenants of the earl or of his barons.

Among Earl Ranulf's own officers, pride of place went to Philip de Orreby, who served as justiciar of Chester - with powers to take the earl's place as head of the county court - from c.1207 until 1229. He was by far the most frequent witness to Ranulf's known charters, with about 100 attestations to his name. They ranged from documents which the earl would have regarded as of great moment, such as the Welsh marriage agreement and grants in favour of the citizens of Chester and the monks of Dieulacres, to routine transactions involving small amounts of property.[162] Another who appeared on the list, though lower down the order, was Peter the clerk, whom we have frequently encountered as in receipt of the earl's patronage; he witnessed about 50 of the earl's known charters and was clearly a valued confidant.[163] Indeed, most of those on the witness list between Walter Deyville and Robert Deyville give the impression of being members of the comital household, either because they bore appropriate titles ('dispenser' and 'butler') or because of their many attestations to other charters, often in company with one another.[164]

---

[162] *CEC*, nos. 258, 377-79, 381-89, 411, cf. e.g. nos. 253-54, 279 (suggesting that he was with the earl in Normandy c.1200), 299, 327, 335; Crouch, 'Administration', pp. 92-93 (where there is reference to Philip's background as a tenant of the earl in Orby, Lincolnshire).

[163] *CEC*, no. 283 (mentioning one of Peter's sons as the earl's godson), cf. nos. 280-82, 284-86; Crouch, 'Administration', p. 88.

[164] Their records as witnesses can be tracked via the index to *CEC*, but see e.g. no. 315, witnessed by (among others) Philip de Orreby, Peter the clerk, Hugh and Thomas dispensers, Walter de Deyville, Norman Pantulf, Richard Fitton, Robert de Coudray, Robert de Say and Robert de Deyville, as well as by Henry de Audley, Joceram de Helsby and Richard de Kingsley, discussed in the main text. Another worth noting is no. 214, which included Philip de Orreby, Peter the clerk, Hugh and Thomas dispensers, Walter de Deyville, Norman Pantulf, Ivo de Kaletoft, Robert de Say and Robert de Deyville, plus

The motte (mound) of Chester castle, built c.1070, with later masonry. The shire court where Earl Ranulf issued his charter probably met in the bailey to the right, between the motte and the river.

Three who immediately followed this group on the list can be identified as junior members of baronial families: Matthew de Vernon from the barony of Shipbrook, Hamo de Venables from Kinderton, Robert de Mascy from Dunham.[165] Several of those who came after them were minor lords, often bearing the name of the principal (or only) manor for which they were a tenant - Pulford, Helsby, Kingsley, Tarvin, Twemlow; among them, however, were a number who at

---

(again) Henry de Audley and Richard de Kingsley. On Fitton and Coudray, see Ormerod, *History of the County Palatine* (1882), III, pp. 552, 354, 356.
[165] Ormerod, *History of the County Palatine* (1882), I, p. 520; III, pp. 252, 198.

some stage held office, including Richard de Kingsley as an hereditary forester and Joceram de Helsby, Lithulf de Twemlow and Richard de Perpunt as sheriffs.[166] The most substantial Cheshire lay landholder, positioned much earlier on the list, was Henry de Audley, another whose frequent charter attestations suggest a trusted household position but a man who had recently been rewarded with a share of the barony of Nantwich, purchased from one of the co-heiresses.[167]Missing altogether from the witness list were the established Cheshire barons, even though men such as Roger de Montalt the steward, Hamo de Mascy, William de Venables and Warin de Vernon frequently attested on other occasions. They all appeared, for instance, as witnesses to several grants to the earl's religious foundation, Dieulacres abbey near Leek, and to others in favour of Peter the clerk, so giving these charters a more distinguished set of attestations overall than the Cheshire Magna Carta itself.[168] However, their omission should occasion no surprise. The various concessions were clearly very important to them and they may well have been present in the county court to observe the formal issue of the charter, but they could not be named as witnesses since - as the opening section of the charter expresses it - they were the declared beneficiaries, at whose petition the grants had been made. Instead of the Cheshire barons, those attesting Ranulf's great charter appear to have been, on the one hand, his trusted advisors and officers (in principle not unlike those named in the king's Magna Carta, though

[166] *CEC*, nos. 213, 241, 249, 261, 275, 283, 371-72, 379, 423; Ormerod, *History of the County Palatine* (1882), II, pp. 62, 72, 87, 90; III, pp. 135, 210 (cf. for Robert de Pulford, Richard de Brescy and Philip de Tarvin: II, pp. 854, 857; III, p. 330; II, pp. 306-7).

[167] CEC, nos. 395-96, and cf. as examples of his attestations among officers and members of the earl's household, nos. 211, 214, 315, 359-60, 374, 379, 381, 384, 408; Ormerod, *History of the County Palatine* (1882), III, pp. 390, 422-24.

[168] *CEC*, nos. 377-79, 282-83, 285. For the baronies, see Ormerod, *History of the County Palatine* (1882), I, pp. 51-52; *Calendar of Court Rolls of Chester*, ed. Stewart-Brown, pp. xlvi-xlvii; *VCH: Cheshire*, I, pp. 310-12.

here of much humbler stock) and, on the other, a selection of others in attendance at the county court: the abbot of Chester, men doing suit to the court on account of their holdings (as described in our discussion of clause 5 above), and those representing their baronial families (whether or not in the capacity of stewards, as envisaged in clause 7). Among the many suitors to the court who could have been named as witnesses, some preference was apparently given to those with a proven record of service to Ranulf III, as sheriff or forester. The message coming through loud and clear was that, notwithstanding these concessions, the earl remained in control.

Summary of the charter

In his commentary on Earl Ranulf's charter for the Chetham Society, James Tait compared it to King John's Magna Carta and declared the Cheshire document to be 'the more rigidly feudal of the two'.[169] This conclusion was based on its lack of concern about wider issues beyond those affecting the relations between the earl and his barons. It is true that the Cheshire Magna Carta offered nothing on the protection of merchants or river navigation, let alone the freedom of the Church, and ventured onto the subject of boroughs only to safeguard barons' rights to reclaim fugitive villeins. It also, of course, lacked the various promises to deal with the immediate political crisis of summer 1215, which dominated the closing section of the Runnymede charter. But anger over unfair exploitation of 'feudal' entitlements, which had fuelled the hostility to King John and which featured in all but the first of the opening eight clauses of his Magna Carta - the charging of excessive reliefs, the abuse of rights of wardship, the mistreatment of heirs and widows in matters of marriage - is scarcely apparent in Cheshire, where one relatively-short clause (no. 8) was sufficient to deal with these issues. This is a charter which implies general acceptance of the barons' relationship with the earl as their overlord.

---

[169] *Chartulary of St Werburgh, Chester*, ed. Tait, I, p. 108.

The barons' chief anxieties - in fairness, also recognised by Tait - stemmed partly from Cheshire's position as an under-populated, under-resourced county on a vulnerable frontier, and partly - against this background of limited resources - from what they perceived as the unreasonable activities of the earl's officers, who levied unfair exactions and took their men into custody: all this in a county where shortage of manpower prevented the full exploitation of arable land, curtailing income from estates, and where the demands of military service were liable to reduce that manpower even further.[170] These were the main sources of friction between the earl and his Cheshire barons and - if we leave to one side clause 8 and the one immediately preceding it about stewards serving as representatives in court - all the clauses offering substantive concessions, from 1 to 11, can at least partly be read in this light.

So we encounter the barons' concerns to ensure that, as far as possible, the residents of their estates should remain within the jurisdiction of their own courts, rather than the earl's, so that they could retain some control over their fate (clauses 1, 4, 6); to assert their own rights - alongside those of the earl - to settle 'avowers' on their estates, as workforce and potential soldiers, and to reclaim villeins living in Chester (clauses 2, 3, 9); to remove restrictions on extending the cultivated area within the earl's forests (clause 6); to define the limits of their military obligations to the earl (clauses 3, 10); and to curb the impositions of the earl's officials (clauses 5, 6, 11 and note also clause 1). The promises which emerged from all this, laced with particulars such as 'thwertnic' and the significance of the Lyme, reinforced the distinctive county identity out of which the demands had arisen. Some of the concessions were probably no more than confirmations of existing practice, others were certainly new. Among them were several which represented extensions to the baronial community at large of what had already been specially granted to a favoured few (clauses 1, 6, 7, 11); there was a parallel

---

[170] On this point, see especially Morgan, *War and Society*, pp. 79-81.

with King John's Magna Carta here, since a culture of selling privileges had developed since the accession of Richard I and the baronage of England had come to think, as Holt put it, 'that what some could buy should be equally available to all'.[171] Collectively, the various clauses offer an insight into the political and cultural aspirations of the landholding class, below the ranks of the great tenants-in-chief and away from the main centres of power, in early thirteenth-century England.

Sequel

On his deathbed, King John dictated a will in which the earl of Chester was named as one of thirteen executors. Ranulf arrived in Gloucester a day late for the coronation on 28 October 2016 of John's nine-year-old heir Henry III, hastily arranged by his fellow-executors, but approved of his colleagues' actions, declined the offer of the regency and endorsed the choice as regent of William Marshal, an older man and the only royalist baron who rivalled him in prestige.[172]

A fortnight or so later, on 12 November, the young king's leading supporters issued a revised version of Magna Carta in his name, renewing and occasionally tweaking the clauses about fair treatment of the barons (including nearly all those quoted above),[173] remitting for further consideration some 'doubtful' ones, such as those which restricted the king's freedom to levy taxes without consent, and omitting altogether the clauses towards the end dealing with the immediate crisis, among them the promise to expel foreign mercenaries and the 'security clause' with its 25 barons empowered to

---

[171] Holt, *Magna Carta*, p. 51.

[172] S. Painter, *William Marshal* (Baltimore, 1933), pp. 192-96; Warren, *King John*, pp. 275-76; D.A. Carpenter, *The Minority of Henry III* (London, 1990), pp. 16-17; D. Crouch, *William Marshal, Knighthood, War and Chivalry, 1147-1219* (2nd edn., London, 2002), pp. 124-27, 167.

[173] Clause 48 about investigations into the evil customs of foresters and others did not reappear in 1216.

coerce the king. This time, Ranulf earl of Chester appeared prominently among the 'noble men', second only to William Marshal among the laity, throwing his weight behind a new role for Magna Carta: no longer a string of concessions extracted from an established king by his enemies but a manifesto issued on behalf of an incomer by his supporters.[174] It is not entirely fanciful to suggest that Ranulf's experience of granting a similar charter for Cheshire, in the routine context of the county court and in a manner which scarcely undermined his authority, was a factor which led him to approve, perhaps even to propose, the reissued version of the Runnymede Magna Carta as a means to bind England to its young king.[175]

Whatever the truth of this, the 1216 Magna Carta certainly played its part in promoting the cause of Henry III. Support for the rebels dwindled, the decisive engagements went in the English royalists' favour and a treaty in September 1217 brought the war to a close. The victory was marked by a further reissue of Magna Carta, again with some adjustments including the removal of matters concerning the royal forests to the separate Charter of the Forest which we have encountered already. Another Magna Carta, further rephrased in places and reduced to 37 clauses, followed in 1225, with Ranulf earl of Chester again one of the witnesses; this stressed that the king (approaching the end of his minority) was making the concessions 'of our own spontaneous goodwill ... to ... all of our realm ... for ever'. It was this version, alongside a new Charter of the Forest, which came to be accepted as the law of the land, repeatedly confirmed by Henry III and his successors and frequently referred to by litigants and commentators alike - although there were to be no further reissues, involving the distribution of fresh copies around the country, after 1300. Despite concerted efforts to repeal Magna Carta's outdated provisions in the nineteenth and twentieth centuries, four clauses from 1215 - safeguarding the freedom of the English church,

---

[174] *EHD*, III, no. 22; Holt, *Magna Carta*, pp. 378-82.
[175] Cf. for a different slant on Ranulf's attitude to the 1216 reissue, Carpenter, *Minority of Henry III*, p. 23.

guaranteeing the liberties of London and other towns, promising judgment by one's peers and according to law, and undertaking not to sell, refuse or delay right or justice - remain (in their 1225 form) as part of English law to this day.[176] In an age of cuts to the legal aid budget and of lengthy waits for cases to come to court, it is worth reflecting on the extent to which this last clause is actually being honoured as we mark the 800th anniversary.

Meanwhile, Cheshire's separatist tradition persisted. Earl Ranulf returned from crusade in the summer of 1220, having been a leading participant in a triumphant siege of the Egyptian port of Damietta. He was received in Chester 'with the greatest veneration as well by the clergy as the laity'.[177] With William Marshal dead, he found himself at odds with the chief justiciar Hubert de Burgh who now became the most influential figure in Henry III's minority government. For the rest of his life, Ranulf was more assertive about his entitlement to pursue an independent line: cementing an alliance with Llywelyn, ruler of Gwynedd, through negotiating the marriage of his nephew and heir John le Scot to Llywelyn's daughter Helen, building Chartley and Beeston castles - controlling access into and through Cheshire from the English Midlands - and (as we have seen, and assuming Barraclough's suggested dating to be correct) forbidding clearings to be made in the wooded Lyme so as not to compromise its defensibility.[178] The earl of Chester never renounced his fealty to Henry III, but his loyalty was that of a baron of immense

---

[176] Holt, *The Northerners*, p. 3 and n. 3; Carpenter, *Minority of Henry III*, p. 288; Holt, *Magna Carta*, pp. 378-405; Vincent, *Magna Carta*, pp. 84-88, 101-102.
[177] *Annales Cestrienses*, ed. Christie, pp. 50-51.
[178] CEC, no. 411; Barraclough, 'Earldom and County Palatine', pp. 52-53, 56-57; R. McGuicken [Swallow], 'Castle in context: redefining the significance of Beeston Castle, Cheshire', *Journal of the Chester Archaeological Society*, LXXXI (2006), pp. 65-82; R. Swallow, 'Gateways to Power: The Castles of Ranulf III of Chester and Llywelyn the Great of Gwynedd', *Archaeological Journal*, CLXXI (2014), pp. 291-314.

wealth and prestige, a 'venerated crusader' who expected to be left free to conduct his own 'foreign policy' with the Welsh and to govern Cheshire without interference. In these circumstances, it is hardly surprising that when Ranulf's death without issue in 1232, followed by that of John le Scot five years later, allowed the honour to be dismembered and the county to be annexed by the crown, the opportunity could not be missed.[179] Cheshire's return to the pipe rolls in 1237 duly signals its recovery by Henry III. In 1254 the county became an apanage for the king's son Edward, who (as Edward I) almost half a century later initiated what developed into a tradition, still observed today, of the title 'earl of Chester' being granted to the reigning monarch's eldest son.

However, the royal officials who moved in to take control of Cheshire left its distinctive institutions largely intact. Barraclough is surely right to claim that it was in the decades after 1237 that a 'palatinate tradition' developed, as local barons argued in defence of established arrangements against the threat posed by imported administrators who had been trained elsewhere. In this quest they were broadly successful. In 1249, for example, after complaints from the 'barons and community' of Cheshire that local customs were not being respected, Henry III ordered that three current in Earl Ranulf's time should continue to be observed; none of the concessions related directly to Earl Ranulf's great charter, but this was in a sense a re-run of 1215, with grievances being openly aired and some - not all - being addressed.[180] Ten years later, there was vigorous opposition in the county court to the authority vested by the future Edward I in his new

---

[179] R. Stewart-Brown, 'The End of the Norman Earldom of Chester', *EHR*, XXXV (1920), pp. 26-53; R. Eales, 'Henry III and the End of the Norman Earldom of Chester' in P.R. Coss and S.D. Lloyd, *Thirteenth Century England*, I (Woodbridge, 1986), pp. 100-13.

[180] *Calendar of Close Rolls, Henry III, 1247-1251* (HMSO, London, 1922), pp. 185-86; *VCH: Cheshire*, II, p. 8. The king's concessions related to matters such as the fixing of the justiciar's court at Chester and limits to certain penalties.

warden of forests, Sir Thomas de Orreby, seen to be usurping the judicial role traditionally discharged by the chief justiciar 'contrary to the laws and customs used in the times of the earls'.[181] By the fourteenth century, the arrangements for governing the county were badly in need of an overhaul, but successive kings had no incentive to make it a priority. Cheshire became known as an unusually-lawless county, a violent threat to its neighbours because of the 'bodies of armed men' who 'committed great robberies' in Shropshire, Staffordshire and Derbyshire before crossing back across the border laden with booty.[182] But it also made a disproportionately-high contribution to royal armies: never more so than under Richard II, who in 1397 recruited a large personal bodyguard from the county and briefly raised Cheshire to the status of a 'principality', with himself as its prince.[183]

After more Cheshire blood had been spilt in the armies of both the Hundred Years' War and the Wars of the Roses, it was left to the early Tudor kings, Henry VII and Henry VIII, to extend the normal machinery of government to the county. Accordingly, by 1543 Cheshire had representation in parliament, was subject to visitations by JPs and (as noted in the commentary on clauses 2 and 4 above) had been deprived of any customary legal peculiarities which set it apart from the rest of the kingdom. The office of justiciar of Chester continued until 1830, but as part of a network applying the standard laws of the land. The Chester exchequer also survived to 1830, but as a court dealing with disputes over debts and other personal liabilities,

---

[181] *Calendar of Court Rolls of Chester*, ed. Stewart-Brown, p. 2.
[182] 'Palatinate of Chester Records Deposited in the Public Record Office: Calendar of Recognizance Rolls to Hen IV', in *Appendix II to the Thirty-Sixth Report of the Deputy Keeper of the Public Records* (HMSO, London, 1875), p. 100; Booth, *Financial Administration*, pp. 7-8.
[183] R.R. Davies, 'Richard II and the Principality of Chester, 1397-99' in F.R.H. du Boulay and C.M. Barron, eds., *The Reign of Richard II* (London, 1971), pp. 256-79; Morgan, *War and Society*, pp. 198-207.

not as a financial office. The last vestiges of the county's 'special status' then came to an end.[184]

As for the Cheshire Magna Carta itself, while Ranulf III saw no reason to renew it, we have already observed that Edward I twice issued a confirmation, before and after he became king; these can be seen as accompanying the reissues of Magna Carta in 1265 and 1300.[185] Following the transfer of lordship over Cheshire to the crown in the 1230s, there was now no question but that the provisions of the king's Magna Carta - the 1225 version - ought now to apply within the county, so the repeated confirmation of a separate Cheshire charter was a signal of continuing distinctiveness. Later sovereigns, including Edward II in the fourteenth century, Henry VI in the fifteenth and Elizabeth I in the sixteenth - notwithstanding the curtailing of the county's privileges by her Tudor predecessors - also confirmed it. This recurrent affirmation of the Cheshire Magna Carta emboldened the barons and other freeholders to make use of its promises. We have previously encountered the men of nine Cheshire townships, in 1285, successfully defending their right to cut oaks in Macclesfield forest without the foresters' supervision, after persuading the justiciar to inspect the charter 'granted by Ranulf formerly earl of Chester and confirmed by the king'.[186] In the following century, both Hamo de Mascy, holder of the estate based on Dunham, and Henry duke of Lancaster, baron of Halton, formally claimed the concessions in clauses 1, 2, 4, 5, 7 and at the beginning of 10 (no service beyond the Lyme) as privileges attached to their baronies; both used phraseology which in many places is identical to that in the great charter, though without mentioning it by name.[187] When in 1357 the landholders of

---

[184] Barraclough, 'Earldom and County Palatine', esp. pp. 38-47; *VCH: Cheshire*, II, pp. 6-41, 56-60.

[185] The National Archives, C66/120, m. 22; *Calendar of Patent Rolls, Edward I, 1292-1301* (HMSO, London, 1895), pp. 499-500; Ormerod, *History of the County Palatine* (1882), I, p. 55.

[186] See the commentary on clause 6, above.

[187] Ormerod, *History of the County Palatine* (1882), I, pp. 526, 705.

Wirral were required to prove their claims to rights in the earl's forest of Wirral, 27 out of a total of 34 specifically cited Earl Ranulf's charter as their authorisation to assart, to cultivate previously-farmed land, to take 'husbote' and 'haybote' and to distribute dead wood beyond their own needs, in terms very close to those used in clause 6; indeed, copies of the original charter and of confirmations by Edward I and Edward the Black Prince were produced as evidence.[188]

Beyond this, there are indications that the Cheshire Magna Carta came to be seen - like its great Runnymede exemplar - as of wider significance than simply a series of 'benefits for barons'. As we saw at the beginning of this discussion, it was described in the 1288 Inquest of Service as 'the great common charter of Cheshire'. The monks of Chester also called it the 'common charter of Cheshire' when they entered it - more fully than most of their collection - into their early-fourteenth-century cartulary.[189] Clearly this was a cherished and widely-known document. It was recognised as the county's own 'great charter' and - as the repeated use of the Latin word *communis* emphasises - one regarded as a charter for the county community as a whole: a guarantee of communal liberties to the people at large and a significant contributor to Cheshire's self-image of independence from the rest of the kingdom.

---

[188] *Cheshire Forest Eyre Roll 1357/61 (TNA CHES 33/6), Volume I:Wirral Forest*, ed. Ranulf Higden Society (Record Society of Lancashire and Cheshire, 2015 forthcoming); we are most grateful for the editor's permission to cite this in advance of publication and to Dr Paul Booth for bringing these references to our attention.

[189] *Calendar of Court Rolls of Chester*, ed. Stewart-Brown, pp. 109, 113; *Chartulary of St Werburgh, Chester*, ed. Tait, I, pp. xxxiii, 101 (where the title is given as 'carta communis Cestrisirie').

APPENDIX

THE LATIN TEXT OF THE MAGNA CARTA OF CHESHIRE

Ranulfus comes Cestrie constabulario, dapifero, iusticiario, vicecomiti, baronibus et ballivis et omnibus hominibus suis et amicis presentibus et futuris presentem cartam inspecturis et audituris salutem. Sciatis me cruce signatum pro amore dei et ad peticionem baronum meorum Cestresirie concessisse eis et heredibus suis de me et heredibus meis omnes libertates in presenti carta subscriptas in perpetuum tenendas et habendas, scilicet:

1. Quod unusquisque eorum curiam suam habeat liberam de omnibus placitis et querelis in curia mea motis exceptis placitis ad gladium meum pertinentibus, et quod si quis hominum suorum pro aliquo delicto captus fuerit, per dominum suum sine redemptione replegietur, ita quod dominus suus eum perducat ad tres comitatus et eum quietum reducat, nisi sacraber eum sequatur.

2. Et si aliquis adventitius, qui fidelis sit, in terris eorum venerit et ei placuerit ibidem morari, liceat baroni ipsum habere et retinere, salvis mihi advocariis qui sponte ad me venerint et aliis qui pro transgressu aliunde ad dignitatem meam venerint, et non eis.

3. Et unusquisque baronum, dum opus fuerit, in werra plenarie faciat servicium tot feodorum militum quot tenet, et eorum milites et libere tenentes loricas aut haubergella habeant et feoda sua per corpora sua defendant, licet milites non sint. Et si aliquis eorum talis sit quod terram suam per corpus suum defendere non possit, alium sufficientem loco suo ponere possit. Nec ego nativos eorum ad arma iurare faciam, sed nativos suos, qui per Ranulfum de Davenham ad advocationem meam venerunt, et alios nativos suos, quos suos esse rationabiliter monstrare poterunt, ipsis quietos concedo.

4. Et si vicecomes meus aut aliquis serviens in curia mea aliquem hominum suorum inculpaverit, per thwertnic se defendere poterit propter sirevestoth quod reddunt, nisi secta eum sequatur.

5. Concedo etiam eis quietanciam de garbis et de oblacionibus, quas servientes mei et bedelli exigere solebant. Et quod si aliquis iudex aut sectarius hundredi aut comitatus in curia mea in misericordia inciderit, per duos solidos quietus sit iudex de misericordia et sectarius per duodecim denarios.

6. Concedo etiam eis libertatem assartandi terras suas infra divisas agriculture sue in foresta, et si landa aut terra infra divisas ville sue fuerit, que prius culta fuit, ibi nemus non crescat, liceat eis illam colere sine herbergacione, et liceat eis husbote et haybote in nemore suo capere de omni genere bosci sine visu forestarii, et mortuum boscum suum dare aut vendere cui voluerint. Et homines eorum non implacitentur de foresta pro supradicto, nisi cum manuopere inveniantur.

7. Et unusquisque eorum omnia maneria sua dominica in comitatu et hundredo per unum senescallum presentatum defendere possit.

8. Concedo etiam quod, mortuo viro, uxor sua per quadraginta dies pacem habeat in domo sua. Et heres suus, si etatem habuerit, per rationabile relevium hereditatem suam habeat, scilicet feodum militis per centum solidos. Neque domina neque heres maritetur ubi disparigetur, set per gratum et assensum generis sui maritetur. Et eorum legata teneantur.

9. Et nullus eorum nativum suum amittat occasione, si in civitate Cestrie venerit, nisi ibi manserit per unum annum et unum diem sine calumpnia.

10. Et propter grave servicium quod in Cestresiria faciunt, nullus eorum extra Limam servicium mihi faciet, nisi per gratum suum et ad custum meum. Et si milites mei de Anglia summoniti fuerint, qui mihi wardam apud Cestriam debent, et venti sint ad wardam suam faciendam, et exercitus aliunde inimicorum meorum non sit in presenti, nec opus fuerit, bene licet baronibus meis interim ad domos suas redire et requiescere. Et si exercitus inimicorum meorum promptus fuerit de veniendo in terram meam in Cestresiria, vel si castellum assessum fuerit, predicti barones cum exercitu suo et nisu suo statim ad summonitionem meam venient ad removendum exercitum illum ad posse suum. Et cum exercitus ille de terra mea recessus fuerit, predicti barones cum exercitu suo ad terras suas redire poterunt et requiescere, dum milites de Anglia wardam suam faciunt et opus de eis non fuerit, salvis mihi serviciis suis, que facere debent.

11. Concedo etiam eis quod in tempore pacis tantum duodecim servientes itinerantes habeantur in terra mea cum uno equo, qui sit magistri servientis, qui etiam prebendam non habeat a Pascha usque ad festum sancti Michaelis, nisi per gratiam, et ut ipsi servientes comedant cibum qualem in domibus hominum invenerint, sine

emptione alterius cibi ad opus eorum, nec in aliquibus dominicis baronum comedant. Et in tempore guerre per consilium meum aut iusticiarii mei et ipsorum, ponantur servientes sufficientes ad terram meam custodiendam, prout opus fuerit.

12. Et sciendum est quod predicti barones peticiones subscriptas, quas a me requirebant, omnino mihi et heredibus meis de se et heredibus suis remiserunt, ita quod nihil in eis de cetero clamare poterunt, nisi per gratiam et misericordiam meam; scilicet, senescallus peticionem de wrec et de pisce in terram suam per mare deiecto, et de bersare in foresta mea ad tres arcus, et de percursu canum suorum; et alii peticionem de agistiamento porcorum in foresta mea et de bersare ad tres arcus in foresta mea, vel ad cursus leporariorum suorum in foresta in eundo versus Cestriam per summonitionem vel in redeundo; et petitionem de misericordia iudicum de Wich triginta bullonum salis, set erunt misericordia et leges in Wich tales quales prius fuerunt.

13. Concedo igitur et presenti carta mea confirmo de me et heredibus meis communibus militibus omnibus et libere tenentibus totius Cestresirie et eorum heredibus omnes predictas libertates habendas et tenendas de baronibus meis et de ceteris dominis suis, quicumque sint, sicut ipsi barones et milites et ceteri libere tenentes eas de me tenent.

Hiis testibus Hugone abbate sancte Werburge Cestrie, Philippo de Orrebi tunc tempore iusticiario Cestrie, Henrico de Aldithelega, Waltero Deyville, Hugone dispensario, Thoma dispensario, Willelmo pincerna, Waltero de Coventria, Ricardo Phitun, Roberto de Coudrey, Ivone de Kaletoft, Roberto de Say, Normanno de Paunton, Roberto dispensario, Roberto Deyville, Matheo de Vernun, Hamone de Venables, Roberto de Masci, Alano de Waley, Hugone de Culumbe, Roberto de Pulfort, Petro clerico, Hugone de Pasci, Joceralmo de Helesby, Ricardo de Bresci, Ricardo de Kingesle, Philippo de Therven, Lithulfo de Thwamlawe, Ricardo de Perpunt, et toto comitatu Cestrie.

(Reproduced by courtesy of the Council of the Record Society of Lancashire and Cheshire from *Charters of the Anglo-Norman Earls of Chester, c.1071-1237*, ed. G. Barraclough, Record Society of Lancashire and Cheshire, CXXVI, 1988, no. 394, pp. 388-91, where notes are provided on minor textual differences between the various copies. We have preferred 'quietos' as the penultimate word of clause 3, as in *Chartulary of St Werburgh, Chester*, ed. Tait, I, p. 103, to Barraclough's 'quietas'.)